"Our American dream of marriage is so idealistic, so romanticized—it is no wonder we have trouble living in the real, everyday world. . . . Even couples who can't remember the romance of the forties and fifties have been sucked in by the materialism of the sixties. Bliss would be a ranch home, a well-manicured lawn, a station wagon with four kids and a dog. What could be closer to heaven than a 'successful' husband who knew how to barbecue steaks on a backyard grill while his lovely wife, fresh from the beauty parlor, poured Pepsi-Cola for the children? What a mixture of romance and despair we live with!"

Charlie Shedd:
"Total communication is where it's at for great marriage. Richard Wilke's book points the way there for any couple who will read and study it seriously."

Tell Me Again, I'm Listening

Richard B. Wilke

PILLAR BOOKS NEW YORK

TELL ME AGAIN, I'M LISTENING

A PILLAR BOOK

Published by arrangement with Abingdon Press

Pillar Books edition published February 1977

ISBN: 0-89129-200-4

Library of Congress Catalog Card Number: 73-3051

PILLAR BOOKS
Pyramid Publications
(Harcourt Brace Jovanovich, Inc.)
757 Third Avenue, New York, New York 10017, U.S.A.

To Julia

*who is patiently teaching me how to listen
and how to love*

Tell Me Again,
I'm Listening

Contents

Preface

If your marriage is like ours, it has been a roller coaster—full of ups and down. At one time or another, we've accused each other of having ears but not hearing. Most husbands and wives, even in solid marriages, miss key signals part of the time. Couples having severe stress suffer this breach even more deeply. Practically every couple who walk through a counselor's door complain about a breakdown in communication. In disgust, she blurts out, "I've told him over and over, but he won't listen." In anger, he cries, "You never hear what I'm trying to say."

It is no secret that marital problems have reached astronomical proportions. Every neighborhood coffee session eventually gets around to the latest batch of divorces. Lots of couples who have been married a long time still aren't sure of themselves. Some young brides and grooms walk across the threshold just plain scared. Even those of us who are finding music and rhythm in our marriages know that every tomorrow is a new challenge to make it work.

Julia and I have been learning in our own marriage for nearly twenty years. We have read the books—everything from Freud to Reubens, from Kinsey to Ann Landers. We have read the Bible. But most of what we have learned has been right in our own living room and bedroom and kitchen as we have tried to learn how to love. We win some great victories together, and whenever we do, the kisses are sweet.

Besides our own experiences, we have also been exposed to the intimacies of other marriages. Like every pastor, I have heard the trembling voice on the phone or the timid knock on the door. Another marriage was out of joint. Ministers and priests are being called on to do a fantastically large amount of marriage counseling. I found myself so deeply involved that I decided to get some additional training. Courses in counseling were helpful at various seminaries. Yale, Dubuque, St. Thomas Aquinas, and Wartburg. For good measure and for practical, everyday experience, I added a day a week in-service at the Menninger Foundation.

Then a few years ago, Julia and I began to develop marriage therapy groups right in our own living room. We met with five or six troubled couples each week for nearly a year. Then we started afresh with another group.

These were husbands and wives whose relationships were distorted. For some, the level of positive dialogue was near zero. Week after week, we sat in a circle around our fireplace, talking and listening, agonizing and exploring. Sometimes the silence was painful; sometimes it was like a prayer. But gradually, individuals began to hear what others were saying. Husbands and wives faced issues that they had ignored for years. The twisted strings of love became untangled. We saw miracles happen. Their doctors and lawyers—especially their children observed dramatic changes.

We came out of those experiences stronger in our own marriage and excited about sharing what we had learned. If we can continue to hear each other's deepest feelings—at least most of the time—and if we can stimulate our readers to explore more profoundly the mystery of dialogue we will be happy.

Richard B. Wilke

1

Moonlight and Roses

The American Dream

It was January. Icy. Windy. The sleet pecked at the windows. Our marriage therapy group was gathered in our home for its regular Wednesday night session. Because it was so cold outside, Julia and I decided to make it as warm as possible inside. I built a roaring fire in the fireplace. We put out crayons, paper, old magazines, scissors, and paste, even some wooden tongue depressors, buttons, and ribbon. Our instructions were simple. Every person was to use whatever materials he wished and express his marriage in graphic form—just the way he saw it. I wish you could have seen our living room! Husbands and wives were sprawled on the floor, hunched over a card table, or drawing quietly in a corner. Some made collages, some drew pictures, one man made an architectural model. Sam, who had been married four times—twice to his present wife, who was the mother of his five children—made a dramatic picture that wrenched our heart strings. Up and down the middle of his white paper he drew a heavy black line nearly an inch wide. On one side of the line he pasted pictures of *his* interests—cars, sports, books. On the other side of the black line he pasted *her* interests—cooking, school-teaching, children. Two people lived in totally separate worlds.

Stephanie drew a picture of a man and a woman reaching out their hands to touch each other, straining, but unable to make it. Pete made a floor plan with tongue depressors. The house had a gate that was open, but nobody would walk through it.

Even though Julia and I were leading the group, we made our pictures too. We have always had our strains and stresses—of late, things hadn't been what you would call apple pie. But still I wasn't prepared for her picture. She leafed through the homemaker's magazines—*Better Homes and Gardens, Ladies Home Journal,* etc. and cut out the most gorgeous pictures she could find. She found pictures of lavish holiday dinners with candles and colorful tables. She cut out a young couple, laughing and running barefoot on the beach. She had a picture of a station wagon full of children with baseball gloves and toothy grins. Front and center was a bouquet of four dozen brilliant red American Beauty roses. She pasted all these pictures into an elegant collage—a dream world of idyllic beauty. But then came the moment of truth. She took a large black crayon and softly smeared the whole collection. From top to bottom she blurred and blackened. The bare feet in the sand, the table for two with candles, the laughing children, and the Sweetheart roses, all went under the dark haze. Like smog over an industrial city, her black crayon told of disillusionment and discouragement, of broken dreams and frustrated hopes.

Oh how we set ourselves up for that kind of disillusionment! Like Humpty Dumpty, we sit on a wall of dream-world romance. Then, like Humpty Dumpty, we have a great fall when we face reality. It happens to practically every couple, although many couples think it happens only to them. What a relief it is in a marriage enrichment group when men and women become aware that their experiences are universal, and they are not alone.

Our American dream of marriage is so idealistic, so romanticized—it is no wonder we have trouble living in the real, everyday world. Most young couples think of matrimony as two people in a canoe on a quiet lake at

night under a full moon. At least the over-thirty genera-
tion started out that way. We were fed a steady diet of
Hollywood musicals. We danced into stardust with Fred
Astaire and Ginger Rogers. Some of us fell in love to
Glenn Miller's "String of Pearls." We were nursed on
Mickey Mouse and Shirley Temple.

Even couples who can't remember the romance of
the late forties and fifties have been sucked in by the
materialism of the sixties. Bliss would be a ranch home,
a well-manicured lawn, a station wagon with four kids
and a dog. What could be closer to heaven than a "successful" husband who knew how to barbecue steaks on
a backyard grill while his lovely wife, fresh from the
beauty parlor, poured Pepsi-Cola for the children?

What a mixture of romance and despair we live with.
What a bewildering set of images we try to live up to.
No society has ever been more sentimental or more bewildered over love. Where would a student of history go
to find such confusion? He might look at Greece when
its golden age was tarnishing into homosexuality. Or he
might spotlight medieval knighthood that made a mysterious cult of virginity. Or he might speak of puritan-
ism when giggles were prohibited, even between the
sheets. But even these moments of history would not be
adequate analogies to present-day bewilderment.

I doubt if any culture has ever talked so much about
love and experienced so little as ours. We have recorded
more love songs, written more true confessions, dissemi-
nated more sex information, filmed more bedroom
scenes, and "scientifically" tested more of the physical
and psychic dimensions of lovemaking than all previous
cultures back to Neanderthal Man. The glorious result
is a nation where one of three marriages is dumped in
divorce; counselors' offices are filled with troubled
people; and the institution of marriage itself is under
serious question. Even some of the experts who write
the sophisticated sex books are not able to make it go in
their own homes.

Our expectations are fantastically high. In bygone days a man was happy to get a good woman who could cook. Lots of gals were satisfied to find a man who would work steadily and come home at night. In many cultures, if a man and a woman could produce a sufficient number of children to tend the land and carry on the family name, it was enough. But not for us: we expect moonlight and roses.

Do you know how we Americans define love? I've been collecting definitions the way a small boy picks up pretty rocks. Here are just a few:

"Love is two hearts beating as one amid stardust."

"Love is an inward inexpressibility of an outward overallishness."

"Life is one thing after another; love is two things after each other."

But this one is best: "Love is a feeling you feel when you feel you are going to feel a feeling you've never felt before."

Even the youth culture of the 70s, whose members ridicule the suburbs and who have seen the big musicals only on the late late TV shows, is infected with its own style of romanticism. With blue denim shirts and sandals, the young turn their backs on materialism. They laugh at stuffy traditional forms. They want a relationship of total openness. But they still believe that love is something you *feel* rather than something you *do*. If anything, their expectations are higher than ever. With a delightful emphasis on love and peace and humanness, they break down all sorts of stultifying structures. But their idealism borders on fantasy. Their hopes for sex are akin to a yearning for salvation. In their concepts of nature, they think more of flowers than they do of tornadoes. In their dreams of love, they think more of freedom than they do of responsibility. They still think that love is something that happens rather than something that is built.

It's almost a religious quest, like looking for the Holy

Grail. They have tried drugs and nature and intimacy, but most often they fail to touch the ground of being. The Beatles, you remember, experimented with drugs in a search for the mystical experience. They traveled to India to sit at the feet of a guru. Then they approached marriage in a similar search for meaning. But to expect a man or a woman to do the work of God is to ask too much. Whether it is within formalized matrimony on one hand, or in a shared, "unencumbered" intimacy on the other, it is sentimental to expect your mate to be the expiation for your sins, the purpose for your existence, and the inspiration for your soul.

Julian Huxley was right when he said, "Wed or unwed, we hold in our minds a particularly American dream of love. It has color (all white and gold), a form (perfectly proportioned) and it shoots off sparks. This sometimes makes it difficult to live in the real world. We believe that romance, a sort of stylish passion, leads to love and happiness. But when and if we find love, we are surprised to learn how complex, how private, and how unlike Cinderella's love it really is."[1]

It is no wonder that disillusionment is a standard experience in marriage. We can only live in a dream world so long. When the bills pile up, when there is a ring around the bathtub, when the liver and onions are burned; then the dream disintegrates into a nightmare. Everything goes thud. When Julia shadowed her dream world, she drew a picture for millions of marriages. And why not? With expectations of fantasy, only a wipe-out can result. Some people have the courage to pick up the pieces and start building a realistic relationship. Some people don't. Some split. Some go on in deadly silence.

The Big Squeeze

We really make it rough on the kids. When Grandpa and Grandma got married, he was eighteen and rented a farm adjoining his father's. She was seventeen but had been practicing her household skills for several years. They got furniture and a team of horses for their wedding. Their sex education on the farm was basic and down to earth. But today we put the big squeeze on the young people. On one hand we try to hold them back. Wait—that's the watchword. Wait until you finish college. Wait until you complete the service. Wait until you get a good job. Wait, wait, wait.

Then we tantalize their sensuality. We encourage them to date at fourteen and fifteen, buy them cars at sixteen, and say "What a handsome couple" at seventeen. They are bombarded by drive-in movies and playboy magaines. It's sex, sex, sex.

We withhold basic responsibilities. Most of them cannot get jobs. Most seventeen- and eighteen-year-old boys are not mature enough to carry the responsibilities of marriage. They haven't had enough practical experience. Marriage is for adults. It requires more maturity, than does driving a car or shooting a gun. The teen-age marriage, often complicated by pregnancy, is the highest possible risk marriage. It has less chance of survival than a soldier on jungle patrol.

It is high time we lessened the gap. On one hand we need to reduce the irresponsible sexual stimulus our society gives the young. Unlimited freedom at sixteen is harmful. Basic skills in human relations must be learned and practiced. Essential commitments and responsibilities need to be taught. Nothing pleases a pastor more than visiting with a nineteen-year-old girl who has had a year of work experience after high school. She is a lot more ready for marriage than she was the year before. A boy who has had service training, work experience, or several years of college is a different creature than a high school boy. At the same time, we have to lessen the wait. In our day of graduate schools and professional training, long military service and possible war conditions, the marriage that is ready, ought to be encouraged. If young men and women twenty and twenty-one and twenty-two years of age see only years of waiting ahead of them, they become frustrated, lonely, and afraid. The idea that you have to finish school first is passé in a day when people go to school all their lives.

Julia and I were told to wait. We went steady a year, we were pinned a year, we were engaged a year. And we were old enough to be married before we met. When it came to communications, we were trying to run in the same place so long, we wore out the ground we were running on.

The Youth Culture

With the institution of marriage in such a bad state, it is no wonder that some young people are calling the form itself into question. Boys and girls who come from nice homes with red rambler roses on white picket fences—but where Mom and Dad hate each other's guts—are going to try some other technique. They know that the power isn't in the form. Plenty of nineteen- and twenty-year-olds do not believe the "big lie." They won't accept Madison Avenue's pitch that if you use the right deodorant, buy a boat, or put the kids in good schools, you will know love and satisfaction. Some kids experience heartache, like a friend of mine who watched his parents come home drunk on Christmas eve, knock over the Christmas tree and fall in a heap of broken ornaments. Lots of young men and women come from homes—good, respectable, church-going homes—where communications are frozen like ice. Others come from broken homes where marriage means a tug-of-war. The rope was cut and everybody fell down.

Whenever I talk with teen-agers about marriage, this feeling always comes out: What assurance do I have that if I buy a bridal gown, have a big church wedding, and you say a bunch of prayers over us, we will have a solid and lasting marriage? After all, there are 20 million divorced people in America who went through some kind of ceremony. Kids keep thinking about ineffective and irresponsible adult behavior in marriages that have been blessed by the church and legalized by society. They are tired of cold and angry relationships, and they are hungry for honest, authentic human companionship. But are they going to find it?

Many of them are willing to experiment, for better or worse. Recently I visited a commune in a large midwestern university town. Most of the evening we sat on the floor, ate gingerbread, and talked. I had a fascinating discussion with a young woman. She was nineteen. She was "married," but not officially. She and her "husband" slept together on a pallet in a front bedroom of the huge communal house, but otherwise shared the total living experience with thirty people. Both came from well-to-do, church-going homes. In high school, Martha had been a cheerleader and an honor student. Martha said that she didn't want Steve to feel that she had a hold on him. They both wanted their relationship to rest on love alone. She wanted him to love her for her own self—not to feel tied down. Later in the evening I asked her how much freedom *she* had. She answered that she had recently made an appointment with a man to spend an hour with him in his bedroom to give her freedom reality. She told Steve what she was doing "to keep everything honest." I asked, "How was the hour?"

Without hesitation she said, "Lousy."

"It's better with your husband?" I pressed.

"That's for sure," she replied, and the conversation was closed.

They were so afraid of hollow forms that they bent over backward to destroy them. They wanted the reality of relationship and not the chains of propriety. I bit my tongue when she talked about an open-ended rather than a closed love. I appreciated her hunger for honesty, but I knew all too well that deep relationships require an absolute commitment. Erik Erikson of Harvard says that a person can experience intimacy if he has "the capacity to commit himself to concrete affiliations and partnerships, and to develop the ethical strength to abide by such commitments even though they may call for significant sacrifices and compromises."[2] Had Martha and Steve, in the secret recesses of their hearts, made that kind of commitment? Maybe. Maybe more than some who stand before the altar. But in actual fact, I think not. Their love still rested on moods and feelings. They expected romance without the roots of responsibility. I fear for their future. If Julia stayed with me only as long as "we felt romantic about each other," as long as things went well, she would have left me long ago. In fact, one night in desperation she said, "Well, I'm stuck with you and you're stuck with me. We might as well make the best of it." That's when our marriage began to click.

That there is a sexual revolution going on in our culture is now completely clear. Some people argue that nothing different is really happening. There's only more publicity to promiscuity—there have always been kids making love in the back seats, they say. Others, including some sociologists, claim that the institution of marriage is moving into something far superior to what we have known in the past. These arguments are hogwash. We are in trouble, and we had better admit it. Every third bride is pregnant when she walks down the aisle. This year will see 300,000 babies born out of wedlock, an all-time high in spite of contraceptives and liberalized abortion. Veneral disease is epidemic. Physicians in small towns as well as big cities receive regular requests for birth control pills from unmarried girls. Pastors and counselors are working with unmarried couples who are living together and experiencing extreme emotional stress.

I'm thinking of Judy and George. They were senior students at a state university. Their marriage was scheduled in six months, but they had been staying together, especially on weekends, for some time. It was very important to their parents that they finish school. George was carrying two jobs, was tired and discouraged. Judy was high strung and nervous, often experiencing headaches and the inability to sleep at night. I asked them why they didn't get married right away. They answered that their parents would be very disappointed. Wouldn't their parents be disappointed if they knew about the present setup? Yes, but the parents were primarily concerned about the education, they felt. They struggled along until their wedding, but they entered it with a trainload full of guilt and anxiety.

The hard core of the youth culture is more hip than all this. Young men and women wander the streets of our cities—many of them the products of sterile homelife. They see each other as ships passing in the night. Relationships are so desperately important and so terribly fragile that communication, even for an instant, is precious. In a world of draft lotteries and war, race tension and broken relationships, love—even for a night —is important. A generation late, they've discovered Hemingway and claim to be the "Now Generation." "That is all your whole life is; now. There is nothing else than now. There is neither yesterday, certainly, nor is there any tomorrow. How old must you be before you know that? There is only now and if now is only two days, then two days is your life."[3]

The Now Generation has a fringe group which has dropped out of all the traditional categories and institutions. Word coming from Europe indicates that three to seven million vagabonds are wandering about the continent. Even experienced journalists are nonplussed by their nonchalant sexual attitudes. "Dudes and chicks," as the sexes are identified, sleep in the same tents, often in the same sleeping bags. Many girls do not even carry sleeping bags.

Martin Luther once commented that mankind is like a drunk peasant riding home on his horse late at night. He was always about to fall off, first on one side and then on the other. Surely freewheeling sexual involvement has as many problems as rigid middle class hypocrisy and prudery. Yet, it is not time for the moralist to get out his Bible and his Boy Scout Handbook and start condemning people. Nor is it helpful to demand that people "get married," as if *that* would solve all of the problems. (Actually, we have become rather famous for electing as president of the local garden club the woman who has slept with a dozen different men but who has a ring on her finger. Then at the same time we thumb our noses at a couple of kids who are trying to learn how to love each other.) It is rather time for people who know the meaning of love relationships to tell the real story. It is a chance for people who know the meaning of dialogue to communicate the truths they have discovered to a needy world. Let the realists come to the fore. Let those whose love is rooted and grounded in an eternal lively love spread the word.

Let the woman who is learning what it is like to share her life with a man who isn't perfect tell her love story. Let her tell it after she has come down out of the rosy clouds and after she has walked through the valley of despond. Let the man who has cooked the meals for his sick, pregnant wife and who has wiped up the vomit tell it the way it is. Let him say how he talked it through with the Lord and with his wife. Leave in all the struggle and the tears, all the defeats and the victories. Above all leave in the *mystery of dialogue*—that strange and wonderful thing some people call understanding, some call communications, and others call love.

Sure, we live in times that can tear marriages to pieces. Freedoms unheard of in earlier eras are commonplace. The woman's role is unclear: she does not know who she's supposed to be or what she's supposed to do. The man's responsibilities are blurred: his leadership is weak and inadequate. Family forms are being altered. The old three-generation style of family is gone. The "ideal" nuclear family—four kids and a dog—is bowing out to ecology-minded couples who think in terms of zero population growth. Medical science provides endless moral choices. Legal and religious forms are scarcely discernible.

But the potential mystery is still there. It is a mystery that is rooted in creation itself. A man and a woman and their mutual needs—that is still with us. The possibility of building a relationship—*that* hasn't been lost. Mature love can come up from the ashes of disillusionment and irresponsibility.

It requires two people who care. It requires two people who care enough to try and fail and try again. It requires a man and wife who will try, in a thousand ways, to say "I love you," and who will engage in a lifetime of effort to understand.

Dialogue Is the Key

How can we be pals
    when you speak English
    and I speak English
    and you never understand me
    and I never understand you?
          —*Carl Sandburg*

Dialogue Is Difficult

Trying to understand each other is tough. It's a goal that has to be pursued relentlessly. The task is one that never ends. It's like golf. Just about the time you think you have got the game in hand, you slice one into the trees or blow a simple putt. You never totally win. You work at it. As in most other important things in life, you may succeed today but you have to do it again tomorrow.

Dialogue is hard for me. By nature I am an introvert, particularly around home. Sometimes I talk to myself. I forget others are around. I have thought that I said certain things, but it only happened in my mind—the words never got out. The mere desire to say something—like having good intentions—isn't good enough. I love to curl up with a good book. When I was a boy I would become so engrossed in reading that I never heard my mother call—not for errands, not even for supper.

Julia is different. Her personality reminds me of Lawrence Welk's music. (She's not square, she's bubbly.) She really emotes. Sometimes I think she lives in a world of feelings. She can talk easily too. The only trouble is, she doesn't always say what she means. Not that she lies. It is simply that her real thoughts are hidden behind the flow of words. After nineteen years of marriage, I am occasionally smart enough to look for the hidden meanings.

For example, we were invited to a party. I came home from work, expecting her to be about ready. She had not started to prepare. She thought we ought to stay home with the children—claimed we had been leaving them too much lately. I reminded her that two of the kids had homework, and the other two were going to meetings. Then she said she had a lot of ironing to do. I could not believe she would give up a party to do the ironing—and I already had a shirt to wear. She mumbled about not having anything to wear, but she was holding up a perfect dress. Finally, at this point, in one of those rare moments when I had enough sense to try really to understand, I said, "Hey Sweetheart, what's the matter?" It was a little thing that was bothering her, but it had loomed large in her feelings. A few tears and an hour later, we went to the party and had a ball. I could not help but think how close I had come to missing the signal.

So many couples never really communicate at all. Or to be more accurate, they communicate only confused or negative feelings. They are constantly defensive. They build strawmen and then knock them down, or else they skim the surface with superficial comments. Positive, understanding just never takes place. They each talk but never hear what the other person is saying.

Some friends of ours, who have a great marriage, are keenly aware of the difficulties of dialogue. He is a busy doctor, she is the mother of three. They have had to work at it, but they've succeeded. Just to remind themselves, they have a motto on their kitchen wall which reads:

I KNOW YOU BELIEVE YOU UNDERSTAND
WHAT YOU THINK I SAID,
BUT I AM NOT SURE YOU REALIZE THAT
WHAT YOU HEARD IS NOT WHAT I MEANT.

The Absence of Dialogue Is Death

It has been scientifically proved that Homo sapiens cannot become human except in relationship with other people. Babies have been brought up in controlled situations where all their physical needs were met, but where they experienced no personal relationships. They failed to develop. Often they became ill and died. Sending out signals and receiving feedback is essential to life. We come into this world hungry to be known, to be heard, to be appreciated, to be loved.

Reuel Howe, in his book, *The Miracle of Dialogue*, writes: "Dialogue is to love, what blood is to the body. When the flow of blood stops, the body dies. When dialogue stops, love dies and resentment and hate are born."[1]

Visit a mental hospital, and you will see some people who have ceased trying to relate to other persons. They have been hurt, so they have retreated inside a shell. The schizophrenic may withdraw into total silence. He still communicates in the sense that he sends out signals—withdrawal, immobility, separateness, aloneness —but he does not experience much dialogue.

Howe means by dialogue a "meeting of meaning." When it is absent, relationships wither. When relationships flounder, people curl up and die. Several years ago I met a sixty-year-old woman who was sailing on a trans-Atlantic ocean liner. She and her husband had separated. She had no children. She had been sailing back and forth for over six months. She bought drinks for whoever would drink with her. She laughed at all the off-color jokes. But she could not establish any relationships. She had no home. For all I know she is still sailing back and forth across the ocean.

When a counselor sees an exceptionally sick marriage, it is like watching a dying man. Dialogue has practically ceased. No longer can the couple express themselves meaningfully to each other. The pain is so severe that they have tried all manner of things to bring some euphoria: separation, heavy drinking, sleeping with other people, going on spending sprees. Anger and resentment seethe beneath the surface. Or sometimes it is a steel-hard coldness, a deadly indifference. In the background there usually are traumatic childhood tragedies like the death or divorce of parents, or broken relationships from previous marriages. In the foreground are twisted thoughts, confused roles, bewildering indecision. They reject their children, yet try to take care of them. The turmoil causes one person to panic, another to withdraw. One person flies into a rage, another flees. Some stay together in mental anguish because they are frightened by the alternative of total aloneness. Inside themselves, they are dying creatures.

In my files are the records of some couples we could not help. Laverna and Larry were one such couple. They asked for help, in a sketchy way, from doctor, attorney, and pastor. But, as with all their relationships, these too lacked trust, commitment, and the willingness to "lay it wide open." Look at this trail of broken and twisted relationships: Laverna's father died when she was a baby; she grew up without a man in the home, knowing neither father nor brother. She became pregnant at seventeen and married. That first husband was a professional military man. They were separated by military assignments. Both ran around with others during the absences. They had three children—seventeen, twelve, and eight—but finally divorced after seventeen years.

Larry had been married before too, right after coming back from Korea. He had been shot in that conflict, paralyzed for nine months, and declared 80 percent disabled. Larry had three boys in that first marriage.

When Laverna and Larry came to me they had been married three years. They came at the referral of Laverna's physician. He had tried about everything medically. She was taking pills to bring on a menstrual period

—a period apparently delayed by emotion. She had been on sulfa for a kidney infection. (Ten years before she had attempted suicide with an overdose of sleeping pills.)

Larry drank too much. Ever since the war he would drink for four or five days at a time. He had some paralysis, but he was filled with self-pity. He expected Laverna to keep track of the finances, but when she overspent, which she often did, he blew a fuse. Recently his fifteen-year-old son had been living with them, and Laverna resented the boy. Larry and Laverna managed to bad-mouth each other at every turn.

The attorney, after two filings for divorce which had been dropped, threw up his hands. The doctor was delighted to make the referral. I met with them several times, individually and togther. But it was very bad. They would not enter our therapy group program— they had so much fear and guilt, it was more openness than they could contemplate. In the counseling sessions they mostly dug at each other, each trying to defend his own little position. They wanted individual interviews so that each one could try to tell me how bad the other was.

Laverna wrote out a note and gave it to me one day. It was a self-evaluation.

As many times as I have asked Larry for his cooperation in not giving the children candy before meals, I still don't have it. I become frustrated at each evening Larry has to be gone from home even though I know there is nothing he can do to prevent it—like Friday, Saturday, and Sunday nights. Wednesday he bowls. Instead of sitting at the table until the meal is finished (till I finish eating), Larry jumps up and leaves to do this or that and takes the kids outside. He doesn't talk to me during meals anyway, so I don't know why it bothers me. When no one is at the table I never finish a meal myself. I feel compelled to get up and clean up the mess even if my plate is half full and I am very hungry.

Without really cancelling, they stopped keeping their

appointments. The last I heard, they had moved to Missouri. Why didn't they split? They were so very helpless, so weak. Yet the fear of being totally alone was even more terrifying than the misery of their staying together. Two lonely, dying souls were limping along together—for a little longer at least.

Dialogue Means Life

It is true that forms of communication are going on all the time—for everyone. We live in a syndrome of communications. We are continually sending and receiving signals. There is a sense in which it is impossible NOT to communicate. A man sitting on a park bench in the warm sunlight with his hat pulled down over his eyes is sending out the message that he wants to be left alone. Sometimes we say of couples in trouble, "They aren't communicating." Actually they are communicating many things—hostility, fear, mistrust, loneliness. But that is not what we normally mean.

We have something much more positive in mind when we say, "Hey, now we're really communicating!" We are thinking of positive responses, of mutual understanding. We mean that we are relating. We look deep into pools of meaning together. There is a meeting. In the church we use the world "fellowship." Sometimes it's corny and superficial; but other times it is profoundly personal. The word comes from the Greek *koinonia,* which means "to hold something in common." In our prayer therapy groups we often felt that we had become little congregations. There was such openness, trust, and concrete sharing of "where we really were." God seems very real when there is a closeness of communications. Dialogue is sacred, spiritual. You want to take off your shoes, for the ground you walk on is holy ground.

Can you remember times in your life when soul touched soul? It represents a time when you shared secret thoughts, and someone understood. Within the black community today, the expression "soul brother" is used. It means that another person—generally another black person—has the ability to understand the meaning of blackness. Actually, everyone wants a soul brother—someone who understands. Each person, in his inner self, craves for others to understand the meaning of his humanness. Specifically each of us wants someone to understand his particular, unique humanness. Christians gain strength from Jesus, who has experienced our human predicament.

In dialogue we open up; commitments are made, relationships are formed, love is born. Twenty years ago I went to Europe on a UNESCO exchange with my two lifelong friends—Peg and Zeke. One night in a little village in Bavaria, after Peg had gone off to her room to bed, Zeke and I took a couple of German porcelain pipes and lit them up. We opened a bottle of Rhine wine the first we had ever had—and we began to talk. We had long pauses. We shared our dreams, our fears, our plans. We talked until four o'clock in the morning. I don't remember the exact content of the conversation, but I know the quality of the relationship. Soul met soul. A friendship was branded into our life-streams that cannot be erased. Although we have been in different parts of the country ever since, whenever we are together for a few hours, it is as if we start in right where we left off.

That is the sort of stuff dialogue is made of.

Husbands and wives ought to be good friends. When I think of my friends, they are all people with whom I have played, or worked, or prayed. With Julia, I have done all three. Emerson's words are even more beautiful when applied to marriage:

Happy is the house that shelters a friend! . . . A friend is a person with whom I may be sincere. Before him I may think aloud. . . . I may drop even those undermost garments of dissimulation, courtesy, and second thought, which men never put off, and may deal with him with the simplicity and wholeness with which one chemical atom meets another.[2]

Those who are afraid that we "will get to know each other too well" fail to understand the unfathomable mystery of the human personality. The more intimate we become, the more keenly we are aware of the kaleidoscopic range of meanings within the other person. Though we spend a whole lifetime "getting to know you, getting to know all about you," we can never know all. What man ever fully understands his wife, or wife her husband, or parent his or her own child? It is a paradox: The more we know, the more beautiful is the mystery.

The Howard Clinebells quote from *No Longer Than a Sigh* by Anne Philipe:

I look at you asleep, and the world you are in, the little smile in the corner of your lips, the flicker of your eyelids, your naked relaxed body, all these are mysteries. I swim at your side in warm transparent water, or I wait for you to appear in the frame of the door under the wisteria. You say good morning and I know what you have dreamed and your first thought at the edge of sleep—and yet you are a mystery. We talk: your voice, your thought, the words you use, are the most familiar in the world. We can even finish sentences begun by the other. And yet you are, and we are, a mystery.[3]

The dialogical effort goes on and on. When the "two become one" they are still individuals, but they combine their time, energy, money, dreams, bodies, and personalities into one mutual effort. It is a sharing, not of halves, but of wholes. Marriage is not a blurring; it is a blending. As the years go by, if the dialogue is continually deepening, everything—from possessions to precious memories—becomes shared ownership. Sandburg sensed it:

What is there for us two
to split fifty-fifty,
to go halvers on?
    A Bible, a deck of cards?
    a farm, a frying pan?
    a porch, front steps to sit on?[4]

Everything, even the mystery, becomes "ours."

The Dialogical Person

What does it mean to be dialogical? It means being
willing and able to learn. It assumes that someone else
has something significant to say. Preachers and teachers,
doctors and judges, even most parents, are often sadly
monological. We tend to be quite ready to give answers.
Sometimes we do not even hear the questions clearly.
"Don't confuse me with the facts, my mind's made up"
is the monological slogan. But the person who knows
how to communicate can learn from a five-year-old
child, a man sweeping the street, or even his wife. Dialogue takes the other person seriously.

It means looking and listening in wonder for exciting
new things. It means standing together in awe, watching
the sun rise. It means pressing your nose against the
glass window in the hospital nursery, hoping to see a
newborn baby yawn. It means holding hands at the annual church Christmas program and listening to the
kindergarten children sing "Away in a Manger."

It means a certain kind of discipline. There are times
when a person has to hold his tongue. The other day
Julia and I telephoned a couple whose son had just died.
We were trying to express our sympathy, but my wife
started off the conversation all wrong. I broke into the
conversation, and after a minute we got it going right
again. After we hung up I started to say, "You really
blew it." You can imagine how *that* would have made
her feel. Instead, I said nothing. Pretty soon, she said,
"I couldn't think. I really said the wrong thing, didn't
I?" I grunted something noncommital. Then she said,

"I sure am glad you spoke up and straightened things out." Boy, did I feel good. Even the blood on my tongue where I bit it tasted good.

Discipline can also mean forcing yourself to say something. It's no good for some tight-lipped character to say, "Well, I just am not very expressive." That is a copout. Even Gary Cooper can say, "Hum, what cha doin'?"

It means a certain openness. People are constantly changing. You are not the same person you were yesterday. That means you cannot peg everything down. Just because she said it last year is no indication that she means it now. In dialogue, husbands and wives are shooting at moving targets while they are on the move themselves. Marriages in which individuals build impenetrable walls around themselves are sick. "I just can't get through to him" are words of frustration.

What hinders dialogue? The "language of love" itself is inadequate. Words are inadequate. Expressions mean different things to different people. Gifts mean one thing but say another. Symbols like food and sex are complicated and confusing. Even a burp can be misinterpreted.

Previous hurts undermine creative communications. The children of unhappy homes are high risk people in their own marriages. They are afraid to develop deep relationships. I tried to help a young married woman named Debbie a short time ago. She was twenty-two, cute as a button, and gave out all kinds of feminine, sexy signals. Inside though, she was frightened to death. Her father had been married four times while she was growing up. She couldn't communicate with her twenty-two-year-old husband at all. A professional psychologist would say she exemplified hysteria—a kind of inner sexual panic. She had never known a man she could trust. The outward flirtation signified a deep inner inability to relate.

Dialogue gets hung-up on self-centeredness. In monologue a person is concerned only with himself. Others exist to serve him. People are treated as things. They are manipulated. They are talked to, or told. One of the long standing jokes in our family is the story about the author who was talking to a lady at a cocktail party. He talked endlessly about himself. Finally, he took a breath and said, "That's enough about me. Let's hear from you. What do you think of my latest book?" Now, in "shorthand," when one of us gets especially self-centered, somebody will say, "What do you think of my latest book." To enter into dialogue, a person has to humble himself, take some risks, be willing to accept the participation of others in his life. A person seeks to give himself to another, and tries to know the other as he truly is.

How can dialogue be developed? Every small-group leader knows that one way to put people at ease and to get discussion going is to admit a mistake, share a weakness, or confess some inadequacy. The rest of the people relax, figuring that they are in the presence of a human being. In our marriage therapy groups, Julia and I would look around the room, see how up-tight couples were as they thought about all their troubles. In the back of their minds they were thinking, "We're in the minister's home. They wouldn't know what trouble is, let alone all the shame, grief, and downright hell we're going through." In the very beginning sessions, Julia and I were not hesitant to tell some of our lonely times, laugh at a sad mishandling of money, admit to breakdowns in communications, express our true puzzlement over raising children. The people became aware that they were not talking with paragons of virtue but with human beings, and they began to open up with their own feelings. One way to develop dialogue is to be honest. When we are honest enough to share our true selves, the sun begins to shine and the kingdom of Heaven is near indeed.

The other night, Julia and I couldn't go to sleep. It was past midnight, and we were tossing and turning. We had drunk too much coffee, were anxious about a number of things, and were generally upset. Before I knew it, she said, "How about a backrub?" I agreed. (Back-rubbing for her is a form of dialogue in which she experiences love and acceptance. She claims it feels good too.) I started reminiscing. I began talking about all the mistakes I had made in our married life. Finally I said that I did not have one single happy memory of anything we had done together our first year of marriage. I remembered a steady stream of term papers, church work, and odd jobs, but I couldn't recall doing anything together that was fun. At that time we had a car, no responsibilities for children, and were in the beautiful state of Connecticut—only eighty miles from New York City. *What had we done with ourselves?* Slowly she began to talk. She remembered night after night when I was studying and she was grading fifth grade arithmetic. She said I was gone several nights a week coaching a church basketball team in addition to the weekend games and youth activities. She sat alone in our tiny two-room garage apartment, homesick, bewildered, and depressed. I asked her why she hadn't said anything at the time to bring me to my senses. She replied that it all took place one day at a time. Besides, she was so unsure of herself as a wife and teacher that she thought it was all her fault.

I began to express how foolish I had been—eighteen years ago. I had been totally unaware of my wife's emotional needs. I had been as insensitive as a telephone pole. I told her how stupid I had been. It was now three o'clock in the morning. We were both deeply relaxed and in each other's arms. Julia's words came very slowly. They came from the depths of her being and printed themselves indelibly on my mind. She said, "I didn't think you would ever understand."

Do you know some dialogical people? I have been keeping my eyes peeled for people who know how to communicate, collecting them into a sort of mental scrapbook. I'm looking for men and women who know how to be fully present, who do not go running off on mental errands. People who share themselves. Recently I met a terrific pastor. He seemed so at ease, so interested in other people. I was not surprised to learn that he had been asked to serve a church of over 3700 members. His name is Stan Brown. He wrote out some of his thoughts on communications—listing his priorities and indicating his views. Here is what he wrote:

I. Talk with God

It is so obvious that I may overlook it. There is the quiet time early in the morning. There is the time of meditation during my study and sermon preparation which is inseparable from an on-going communion with the Spirit. He speaks through the moving pen almost faster than we can formulate the words! There is prayer with other persons in the normal course of a day. How often in a hospital or a home I will say secretly to myself, "What can I do here? This problem is too great for me. I am not able to add anything to the wisdom or the deed." Then I remember: I can pray! I can talk with God and thereby make his presence much more a conscious reality for this person and for me as well.

There are many times I am alone and on my way—to a meeting, to a crisis, to a speaking engagement, to my own home. I must talk with God on the way, asking for power, for clarity, for love, for openness, for understanding, for forgiveness—the list is unending. So my talk with God is unending, and much of the time I just praise him and thank him!

II. Talk with Wife

She shares my ministry as well as my life and person. God has given her to me, and our children—given us all to one another to make our lives complete and more abundant. His love is made known in the midst of us, and we reach out in that love to include others—reach out from the soul of our marriage where God dwells incarnate. If I do not spend time with her, and with our children, how can that love grow? Love must grow or wither. She, and they, are also my parish. Their needs are no less real than those of my congregation, and my calling is to serve them as well. My love for her is to be as sacrificial as Christ's was for his church and as incarnate, as real and involved. He will speak to me often through her, but if she and I do not talk, I will not get the messages. She will wait for the sound of my returning step, and I will share what God has done with me while we were apart. If I do not talk with her my ministry will be mine only; she will be cut off from that which is so important to me, and thus we will be separated from each other in a major area of our lives. Sometimes, often, we will go away alone, even if it isn't far, and just be together and grow quiet in God's love together.

III. Talk with People

To talk is a two-way street. I will listen. My talking is really only between my listening. Even my listening is talking. It is saying "I care about you; you are important. God loves you and I love you. See my eyes looking into yours. See my tears well up with yours. Feel my hand reach out for yours, and the strange peace between us. It is the Presence. It is Jesus. He is here."

They have problems for which I do not have the answers. I tell them so. But between us there is Jesus. We talk about him, and in wonderful ways beyond our understanding, he provides the answers.

My friend added this postscript:

I suppose there are other things in the life of a pastor, maybe some of them that are also important. Right now I can't think of what they might be.

I know of few people who understand love so clearly in terms of dialogue. Unlike a lot of us, he practices what he preaches. He maintains a kind of vulnerable openness which is incarnate agape. Is it any wonder he has a harmonious staff, a growing spiritual church, a solid family life? They key is communication of the inner self.

The Third Ear

The Art of Being Fully Present

Dr. Theodore Reik uses the phrase, "the third ear."[1] He means by it, the ability to "hear" meanings and feelings that are hidden behind words and actions. It requires acute awareness, an empathy with another person, and a keen effort to understand what he is trying to say.

Do you remember when we were kids the schoolteacher would call the roll? We were supposed to answer "present." If nobody said anything, he was presumably absent. I remember once, sitting and daydreaming while the teacher repeated my name. Finally she said, "Dick, are you here or not?" That's a good question in human relations. How present are you when someone is trying to communicate? I know one fellow who is already thinking about what he is going to say while you are still talking. That is one reason we get answers to questions that were never asked. If someone is not listening to you when you are talking, don't you immediately feel angry or frustrated? I do.

The other day I suddenly became as angry at Julia as I have just about ever been. It was not a seething, slow-boil kind of anger. It was like the shot of a rifle. Here is what happened: It was midafternoon. The kids were gone. For some strange reason there was a lull. We decided to drink a cup of coffee together and just visit. I started to tell her about an overseas trip I had been dreaming about. I had been thinking about it for a long time. Now I wanted to sell her on it. I had just warmed up to my subject when she said, "Put a magazine under that cup of coffee before you set it on the end table." I was furious. I told her I would buy her a new table, and the coffee was not fit to drink anyhow. The conversation was over.

Now what had really happened? Apparently I had the feeling that I was sharing a deep part of myself. But evidently she thought we were just passing the time of day, and there was no reason to ruin a perfectly good table. Without telling her, I had made myself extremely vulnerable. I had secretly wanted her to be totally present, fully attentive to my feelings and thoughts. When I felt she wasn't, I was devastated.

Of course, I do not listen too well myself sometimes. Our older daughter, Susan, likes complete attention. It is not unusual for her to yell, "Daddy, you're not listening!" I daydream about things, or sometimes I glance at a newspaper while someone is talking. The other day my son Paul stopped me short and said, "Dad, I want to talk to you for a few minutes, and I don't want you to read or think about anything until I'm through."

That helped me snap to, because Paul gave me a signal. "Hey," he implied, "I'm about to say something important." Julia and I have started to give signals intentionally before we launch into matters where we have a high emotional investment. For example, we will say: "There's a matter we need to think through. Do you have anything else on your mind right now?" Or, "There's something I've been thinking about for quite a while, and I want to talk about it when you have time." It is a lot better for people to know what is going on, even if you have to draw pictures, ring bells, or flash lights to get their attention.

Most of the time we are not trying to impart information so much as we are struggling to explain "where we are." Everybody, deep down, wants to feel that somebody understands. It is a great compliment when someone tells you, "I think you really do understand." Husbands and wives need to keep the antenna up, ready to be completely aware at a moment's notice. You never know when the signal will come.

Children, of course, need a parent's complete attention every now and then. A friend of mine takes one of his daughters with him every few months in his regular daily routine. He is a salesman-businessman, and he takes her from place to place, introducing her, explaining what he does, and visiting along the way. They have lunch together downtown. He shares something of himself, and has a little extra time to listen to one youngster alone. They have a great time.

Think how many skinned knees are "healed" when Mom looks at it, gives it her undivided attention, and kisses it where it hurts. It takes only a few seconds, but it works, if she is fully present for a moment. James Thurber has written somewhere, "Let us not look back in anger, nor forward in fear, but around in awareness."

Dr. Howard Hendricks of Dallas is a fascinating lecturer on family life. He told this personal story not long ago. His son, now nearly a grown man, and he were talking one night. Dr. Hendricks asked him what were some of his fondest memories of childhood. After a moment, the young man said, "Dad, it was the night you fixed my bicycle." Dr. Hendricks couldn't even remember the incident, so his son recalled it for him. One night, years before, the professor had come home from the university and had only a few minutes to get dressed for a dinner speech that evening. As he drove in the driveway, he saw his son sitting on the ground beside his bicycle, anxiously waiting for Dad to come home. The handlebars on the bike were crooked, and the front wheel needed alignment. For some strange and wonderful reason, Hendricks asked his wife to call the chairman of the meeting and say he would be late. Then he slipped on his old clothes, and for the next half hour, he tinkered with a beat-up bike and enjoyed the company of his son. He was late for the dinner—the chairman had apoplexy when he heard the excuse—but it was worth it. Think of all the hours he had spent with his son across the years. Yet the memory which came most readily to the mind of a nearly grown man was the thirty minutes his dad had taken from a full schedule to give his total, undivided attention.

Do you have agenda-itis? Are you always organizing tomorrow so that you can't experience today? Some folks always try to be in two places at the same time. Others are always wanting to "get on with it." I know one man who usually ruins the family picnic because he has determined in his own mind that they will all leave the house at 3:30 p.m.. At 3:33 p.m., while his wife is frantically packing pickles and putting in a sweater for the baby, he's honking the car horn and smoking at the ears. He doesn't have a blessed thing to do for the rest of the day, but he's so agenda-oriented that he loses human sensitivity.

Dwight D. Eisenhower was a master of the creative use of the present. Maybe it was nurtured in his Quaker home in the quiet town of Abilene. Or maybe it was a discipline learned at West Point. But I have always admired the way he could command an army and still enjoy a dinner with friends. He could lead a nation and have time for a round of golf. He could run a university and take a long walk in the woods with Mamie. If only husbands and wives would learn how to enjoy the precious moments together, married life would be a lot more fun.

What Is He/She Really Saying?

I guess that as long as there has been man, there has been language. Words are necessary for human communication. Words are not the whole story, but they are

essential. Have you ever tried to think without words—
I mean without using words in your mind? It cannot be
done. When the Bible wants to describe God's creative
activity, it says, "In the beginning was the Word." We
cannot intentionally act without thinking, and we cannot think without words. We are always less than adequate as human beings if we cannot express ourselves
with words. Even those who are "men of few words"
simply give added weight to those words they *do* speak.

I remember dating a girl once who never said a
word. She was a beautiful girl. She loved to dance.
She enjoyed cuddling up. But I never knew much about
her. It wasn't so much that she was a woman of mystery
—it was more that she was a woman of "blah." Now,
I'm a great believer in *unspoken* communications
(probably the most important communications are nonverbal), but who wants to be married to a sphinx?

Have you ever heard about the proverbial Vermont
farmer? He claimed that he loved his wife so much that
it was almost more than he could do to keep from telling her! Somehow America has trained a generation of
men in the image of Gary Cooper and John Wayne.
Much of the time our romantic language consists of a
guttural utterance. It is actually amazing how many
men find it difficult to say the magic words, "I love
you." One man had been married over forty years. In
all that time he had never said it. Finally his wife ex-
ploded: "You've never told me you loved me!" It is
reported that he answered: "I told you when we got
married that I loved you. I also told you that if the
situation ever changed, you would be the very *first*
one to know."

I will never forget the night Harry learned how important it was to say it with words. Harry was one of
those fellows who never said many words that carried
emotional material. He was articulate in talking about
facts and figures, but he was a mummy when it came
to feelings. His wife never knew what he was feeling

deep inside. When Harry and his wife entered one of our therapy groups, the gulf between them was as wide as the Grand Canyon. He sat through the first half dozen sessions without speaking.

Then one night the group started talking about this very subject—the importance of reassurance, of saying actual words of affection. The women grabbed the issue like bass hitting the lure. They told how important it was for their husbands to say the simple words, "I love you," *every day*. Out of the corner of my eye, I watched Harry as he began to listen intently. His wife, Beth, watched him out of the corner of *her* eye. Finally one woman who sat across the room from him really let it rip. She gave a three-minute oration: "Don't you fellows realize that we gals clean house and cook and put on perfume and change the diapers and put flowers on the table and do about everything else we can think of just to get a simple word of assurance that you care? Don't you realize that we *live* for words of affection from you bums? And we want to be told every day—several times a day if possible—that you love us."

It was as if Harry had heard something for the first time in his life. Very softly, but quite clearly, he said, "My wife has been trying to tell me that for years, but I didn't believe her. I didn't realize it was *that* important." Beth, meanwhile, was wiggling with excitement. "A thousand times I've told him! He had to hear it from somebody else!"

Now men need words of love too. And some women are as tight-lipped as any man. Others say lots of words but never say the right words. A man can die of thirst in a sea of irrelevant words—waiting with parched lips for an honest word of appreciation and affection.

But words are tricky. Words have different meanings to different people. Besides, in any given social context, there are levels of meaning. Sometimes the words simply come out wrong—or with double meaning. A friend of mine, a social worker for county welfare, has collected some interesting letters that were received asking for financial support. Just for fun, here are some of them:

One woman wrote: "This is my eighth child. What are you going to do about it?"

One report indicated: "Mrs. Jones has not had any clothes for a year and has been visited regularly by the clergy."

Another woman said, "My husband got his project cut off last week, and I haven't had any relief since."

The letter said, "I want money as quick as I can get it. I have been in bed with a doctor for two weeks and he doesn't do me any good. If things don't get better, I'll have to change doctors."

Obviously, the words do not always mean what we want them to mean.

Even if the words are clear, there are feelings behind the words. There are moods and inflections and hidden implications. Some things are said with the head and some things are said with the heart. When you remember that the sender and the receiver may not be on the same wave length, it is no small wonder that we have trouble understanding one another. Douglas Steere says that "in every conversation between two people, there are always at least *six* people present: What each person says are two; What each person meant to say are two more; What each person understood the other to say are two more."[2]

I will not forget an experience when I worked as a teamster in New Haven. For a summer, I worked on the trucks—freight, furniture, and heavy rigging. That was an education every ministerial student ought to have! Most of the drivers were second generation Italian. They were hard-working, hard-talking men tough outside but warm inside. I came to love them in a special way. One day a veteran driver and I were taking a truck load of freight through the center of town. Suddenly he slammed on the brakes and started swearing at the driver of a truck coming from the opposite direction. That driver stopped too. The language they used was an interesting mixture of American and Italian—plus other words whose derivatives I did not know. I watched as the traffic backed up for two blocks in both directions. I looked at the huge driver in the other truck. I flipped the lock on my door and took notice of a pipe wrench lying on the floor board. With mixed feelings, I saw a cop walking toward us from a block away. Suddenly both trucks started up and both drivers began to laugh like crazy. My driver turned to me and, though he was laughing so hard he could hardly talk, said, "That guinea is my cousin."

I learned some important things about communications that day. How could I have known that a couple of grown men had a rather unique and beautiful way of saying "I love you" right in front of the Taft Hotel? I have never called a man a "guinea" and I never intend to. But if I ever should, I hope he's my cousin.

Marriages are like that. An outsider can never really know what is actually being said. One man may light up a cigar when he is happy; another will fog it up when he is mad. One woman will cry when she is lonely and wants attention; another when she wants to be left alone. The trick is deciphering the secret signals. The tragedy is that too much of the time the husband and wife are not even *understanding each other*. A man may say that he is too tired to go bowling; so his wife assumes that he wants to go to sleep. Or the little woman exclaims that she would give anything for a maid; what she means is that she would like for somebody (her husband especially) to notice that she has freshly waxed the kitchen floor.

Let me give an analogy. When I was a young pastor, I was terribly upset that members of the church would go to the hospital and never let me know. I put in the parish news that they should call me so that I could come and see them. Instead, they seemed to make a little game out of it called, "I'm very sick—let's see if you find out about it." Some would let me know, of course, but they were usually the very faithful. Those I would have found out about anyway because they were so often at the church. I quickly learned, however, that many of the people who did not call were really saying, "I want very much for people to love me, to care whether I live or die. I wonder if I have any friends who will care enough to ask the pastor to call on me. I wonder if *he* knows that I exist? I wonder if he will search me out and come to see me?" In actual practice, some of my most significant pastoral calls have been made when some strange combination of circumstance or Providence has taken me to a bedside I *didn't* know existed. The pastor who thinks people are saying "I don't want you to come" will usually be missing the signal. He may even be angry and lose an opportunity. But the priest or minister who hears in the silence the cry of loneliness, knows that being a detective is part of the job.

It takes a lot of detective work in every marriage. I have mentioned some of the curves my wife throws me in terms of *her real* meanings. I am not even aware of most of *my own* bewildering signals. Take a look again at Harry and Beth. Harry is a hard worker. He is a professional man and often works far into the night. When he does come home, it is often late. He is quiet, tired, and hungry for appreciation and affection. Beth, his wife, is a high strung perfectionist. She yearns for approval but never feels that she receives it. Now, take a look at the bedtime signals. Harry works late (can't you just hear the parent in him saying, "Work hard Harry, that's a good boy!"), and he comes home wanting to receive quiet, gentle "stroking." Beth, meanwhile, thinks that if he really loved her, he would have come home earlier and paid her some attention. She keeps looking at the clock and gets tense and angry. Now they are together—two people who love each other very much. She wants him to say, "I'm sorry for being so late." He hopes she will say "Sweetheart, you shouldn't work so hard." She wants him to reach out and take her hand, ask about her day, tell her he loves her—do anything but turn on the tube or pick up a paper. But Harry is afraid. He does not really know how to say all that. Both are sending out signals, "I want to be loved." Neither is able to send out the message, "I love you." Before long, Beth takes a drink, hoping to calm down. Harry interprets this as rejection. He says something critical and she's devastated. Another stiff drink and she goes to bed, hungry for his arms and his kisses. Angry at her and frustrated by his own inability to provide the affection his wife needs, Harry decides to work for another hour or two. Or he drives to another city so he can make an appointment early the next morning. What a fantastic, unfortunate game of hide and seek.

Beth and Harry spent eight months in one of our marriage therapy groups, learning to listen with the third ear, each trying desperately to hear what the other was saying. For two hours on Wednesdays, they tried to be fully present with each other. They kept on trying when they were at home together. Gradually some beautiful and exciting things began to happen in their level of communications. They learned not only to say "I love you" with words, but also to say it in such a way that they could really "hear" it.

Psychiatric Care—Homemade

Not too long ago, a twenty-one-year-old girl graduated from the University of California in sociology. As an experiment in urban sociology—without explaining it to the management or to the customers—she took a job as a barmaid in a West Side New York "dive." "The stools were patched, the neon light was cracked, the drinkers seemed tired, dusty and lonely," she said.

Her name was Astrid Huerter. Her plan for the summer was to experience life as a barmaid, to study the drinker, the decadent neighborhood, and to evaluate the effect the entire situation had on loneliness. "Most of the regular patrons, she said, came to the bar not out of a need to drink or to pass the time of night; but they came rather 'out of a desperate need to communicate with someone and a desire to be heard.' If it was merely alcohol that they wanted, they could have got it at half the price from a liquor store; and if they wished merely to pass time, they could have gone to the movies. . . . But only in the neighborhood bar could they be certain of being heard." It became apparent to Miss Huerter that her real job was to be a professional listener. She said, "In New York . . . people do not have time to listen. Here everything is 'getting ahead' and 'progress' and 'money.' Here you have to *pay people to listen. And that is what a barmaid does.*"[3]

Loneliness is not limited to New York. It lurks in the living rooms and sleeps between the sheets all across the land. It has been only a few short years since the Beatles touched millions of responsive feelings in the youth culture with their hit, "Eleanor Rigby,"

> All the lonely people
> Where do they all come from?
> All the lonely people,
> Where do they all belong?[4]

That is why we need so many professional listeners. Barmaids and doctors, desk sergeants and pastors, lawyers and counselors are paid to listen. A while back, a middle-aged man came into my study to talk. For sixty minutes he poured forth his feelings about his professional anxieties. When he stood to leave, there were tears in his eyes. He shook my hand vigorously, thanked me with warmth, and said, "You've really helped me, and I'm grateful." After the door closed, I thought about our hour together. I realized that I had scarcely uttered a word. I had not offered a prayer, stated any Scripture, or given any profound advice. The full extent of my conversation had been nods and guttural nonverbal utterances. (One psychiatrist claimed that it took him several years to learn to say "uhmmn" so that it meant, "I hear you—I'm not condemning you— please go on.") All I had done was to try to get inside his feelings, hear him out, and sort of agonize with his fears and frustrations. The solution to his dilemma seemed to dawn within him. The burden he carried was lifted by a power beyond us during the encounter.

Some weeks later, that man, with all his education and sophistication, saw me on the street, hailed me and said, "I can't tell you how much you helped me the other day. I didn't think that anyone could understand the feelings I had, but I felt that you did. I made the decision we talked about, and everything is fine."

Now lots of that kind of listening ought to go on within a marriage. Oh sure, it would be a wrong impression to indicate that every marriage could carry the full weight of mutual understanding. I know that there are times when the objectivity of an outsider or the skill of a trained person is necessary. There are illnesses too complicated and crises too traumatic for the marriage partner alone. But it would not miss the mark too far to say that most professional counseling would disappear if there was adequate listening at home. We discovered in our marriage therapy groups that people not only learned to talk, they also learned to listen. One couple even admitted that part of their therapy was getting in the car, driving forty miles to our Wednesday night group, and driving back home. They said they hadn't been together—alone—to talk one night a week for years. If they had done that on a night-out-together basis ten years before, they would not have ever been in the group.

Julia and I have learned to say to the children,

"Leave us alone for a few minutes, we need to talk." We are not afraid to stay up another half hour to bring each other up to date. We try to have an evening once a week that belongs just to us.

One of the problems, of course, is that both husband and wife need to be heard. Both need to be understood. There are men who will read this and say, "Dadgumit, that's right. If only the old lady would listen once in a while." And there are wives who would agree with my thesis, sob softly, and say, "If only he wouldn't clam up when I try to tell him something." It is the old problem. Each of us wants to *be* loved so desperately that we don't have any energy left to *do* any loving. He wants her to listen to him, and she wants him to listen to her. That develops into a Mexican standoff. The only person you can ever expect to change into a more sensitive person, a better listener, is yourself.

Let me tell you about Sam and Kathy who were in one of our groups. Sam was out meeting the public all day. When he came home at night, he wanted peace and quiet. Kathy was home with three little children and the closest she came to adult conversation was drinking coffee with a gossip next door. When Sam came home at night, Kathy flipped a mental switch and gave a running accounts of the day's activities—diapers, spilt bottles, minor neighborhood scandals. Sam barricaded himself behind the newspaper or in front of the TV—protection from the deluge. They hurt each other's feelings every night. Sam accused her of chattering like a magpie; Kathy claimed he was a bore and didn't care about the children.

One night in our group, Sam said something important. "You know what I really enjoy? When I come home, I love the little noises that come from the kitchen while Kathy fixes supper—the smell of the food cooking—the peace of being home—all make me feel good." Then he actually unlocked a door with words that made an opening in a twelve-year wall of hostility. "I wouldn't mind listening to Kathy—even hearing about the daily activities of the children and the problems of the house, *if only she'd wait 'til after supper*." Somehow, for the first time, Kathy heard his inner plea. Several weeks later, they shared with the group that they had made an agreement: Sam had one hour to unwind—an hour of relative quiet while Kathy fixed supper. There was no significant conversation. During supper they chatted with the children. Then, they tucked the children into bed, sat down for a second cup of coffee, and visited about the day's activities. Sam even started drying the dishes. They learned to talk all over again. When bedtime came, the air was clear, the "housekeeping" words had all been spoken. Sam and Kathy could climb into bed and communicate with nonverbals.

Surely God intends for every husband and wife to be a psychiatrist—at least for each other. A personal physician, right in our own homes! We wouldn't have to pay forty dollars an hour either. Actually we ought to be worth more than that to each other. We ought to do a better job than a counselor could do. The doctor normally cannot hug us and kiss us and rub our backs while he listens. He cannot kiss the tears out of our eyes or go to bed and make love as the feelings are being vented. (I did just read an article in a popular magazine. It told about patients who sleep with their psychiatrist and call it therapy. I think it's bunk. So do the reputable professional doctors.. Besides, I don't know any women psychiatrists.)

If one of our deepest needs is to be understood, who is more readily accessible than the man or woman we live with? Those of us who do counseling work know that we are usually picking up the broken pieces that have fallen at home. Careful, empathetic, reflective listening by husbands and wives is the best preventive medicine in the world. (It teaches you to listen to your kids, too. And that is no small matter either.)

One reason group therapy is so useful is because the group is a simulated family. A trained counselor can help people who are not experiencing clear family dialogue relearn and reexperience channels of communications. A truism among therapists is "by the family you have been broken, by the 'family' you will be healed." Married couples groups—even entire family groups—are now not uncommon. People learn what they needed to know earlier—the keen art of hearing. Jesus once said, "He who has ears to hear, let him hear" (Matt. 11:15).

4

Eyes and Sighs

Nonverbal Communications

So far we have placed a great emphasis upon words. It is true that some of us will work like troopers to hear Father (or a father image) say the simple words, "Well done." I had rather have my daughters say the words, "I love you, Daddy," than give me an expensive gift. Many a marriage has been saved from disaster when a husband or wife has the humility to mumble, "I'm sorry." I have seen a counseling session clouded with gloom, then suddenly break wide open when someone angrily blurted out, "Damn it, if I didn't love you so much, I'd have left you a long time ago."

But words, important as they are—even with their emotional overtones—are not the whole story. So much is said sublingually. When it comes to feelings, the most powerful conveyances can be nonverbal: posture, gestures, facial expressions, voice inflections—even the cadence of the words themselves. I know of at least two ways to say, "Did you close the door?" There is a language deeper than words—more primitive than syntax and vocabulary. A wink can say more than a thousand words. A yawn can terminate a party. A sigh can signal a romance. A tear can reveal a broken heart.

I dream on words and lick them
And wonder

How old they are and
>   Who created them
When they were only grunts and groans?
Sometimes I'd rather grunt
>   Than talk
Because words belong to someone else.
My grunts are my own,
>   Lusty in my throat,
>   Strong in my chest,
>   Born in my belly.
Sometimes I'd rather scream than sing
>   Because I write the lyrics
>   To my screams.

Will you come tonight
>   And listen
To my symphony
>   Of grunts and groans and weeping.[1]

The grunts and groans are primitive; but the meanings are not always clear. As with words, the sender does not always convey the same meanings as those understood by the receiver.

Certain actions mean different things to different people, too. Often we say one thing with our words then proceed to contradict with our behavior. It is all part of this complicated process called understanding.

What does it mean when Jack comes home from work and Jill is still in her bathrobe? It could mean a lot of things. What does it mean if Jack stops off for a few beers before he comes home? Nothing? Everything? What does it mean when the little woman suddenly decides to go to the beauty parlor and "get the works." Is she depressed and wants an emotional lift? (Julia gets blue if she thinks her hair looks dowdy.) Is she hinting for a night out on the town? Or is she trying to say, "I'm just as pretty as your secretary"? Who knows what that combination of torture chamber and Swedish massage is designed to do! But it's a wise husband who tries to figure it out.

Why did he leave his dirty socks on the bathroom

floor? Is he just absent-minded? Did his mother always pick them up, and he assumes that his wife is just like good old Mom? (Maybe she actually enjoys mothering him, and they have a kind of a thing going.) Or does he know that socks on the floor will make his wife as mad as hops? By leaving them there, he can smack her one wtihout even raising his voice or lifting a finger.

Psychodrama—a method of therapy—takes bodily manifestations very seriously as meaningful communication. For example: A man sits leaning back, with his arms folded and his legs tightly crossed. His barriers are up. He is defensive. He doesn't want to get involved. The counselor accepts this action as communication and helps the man talk about it. Or a sophisticated woman sits completely relaxed, it seems, smiling and composed. But her right hand tightly squeezes a tiny handkerchief. That small fist, half-hidden between her body and the chair, gives the scarcely perceptible signal that she may be the most anxious person in the room. The therapist, who is trained to spot such nonverbal signs, may ask her to "be her hand." He asks her to let her whole body and personality reflect the feelings of her hand. She may temporarily deny that she is at all anxious or afraid, claiming either that she was not really squeezing her handkerchief, or that it is a meaningless little habit. But with some encouragement, she may be enabled to act out her fright, or she may be able to say in words what her hand has been saying all along.

The intelligent couple learns to interpret fairly accurately the nonspoken signals in their marriage relationship. They even try to use them to good advantage. There is a secret satisfaction in successfully being a Sherlock Holmes on a given case. Big John has a cold, stays home from the office, gets in bed with a hot-water bottle on his feet. He does not say it, but secretly he wants his wife to bring him a glass of orange juice or a cup of hot tea—just like Mother used to do. A degree or two of temperature, and he has reverted to being a little boy again. (There's a little boy deep down in every great big husband—most wives know this.) A smart wife picks up the signal, babies him for a few hours, and soon he is well. Day after tomorrow, he will stick a cigar in his mouth, hustle off to outsmart the competition, and loudly claim that anybody who would let a little cold get him down is a sissy.

Symbols

Symbols have fantastic emotional power. Take patriotic symbols for instance. Some friends were recently telling me about a couple who did not stand at a basketball game when the Star Spangled Banner was sung. My friends were so distraught they could hardly talk about it. Or take religious symbols. A few years ago when guitars were beginning to go to church, we organized a folk choir. One lady, who had helped to buy the pipe organ some years before, walked out in a huff. To hear her tell it, you would have thought Paul walked around the Mediterranean with a pipe organ strapped to his back.

Symbols in marriage are dynamite too. Take the tube of toothpaste. I serve as a counselor for Dr. Crane's Scientific Marriage Foundation—the group that tries to help single adults find a partner. Would you believe that one of the key questions asked on the personality inventory—the information that goes into the computer —is: "Do you squeeze the toothpaste in the middle, or do you carefully roll it up from the end?" That is a dead serious question too. Marriages have smashed up over a tube of toothpaste. (My wife and I are both grab-and-squeezers.)

The family checkbook can be a godlike symbol. Who writes the checks? Does *he* pay all the bills and "give" his wife a few dollars allowance? (One man said his wife was always asking for money. "That keeps you broke," his friend replied. "Oh no," the man answered, "I never give her any.") Or does she take care of the family finances, letting it be well known that if she *didn't,* everything would go to pot? Most couples who fight over money think that if they had more, the problems would end. The truth is, and it has been statistically supported, the amount of money has nothing to do wtih the amount of fighting. It is just as easy to argue over a Rolls Royce as it is a new hat.

One reason priests and preachers are slow to encourage mixed marriages (religious, cultural, racial, educational, geographical) is because symbolic meanings play havoc with the marriage. I could give a score of examples. Recently I attended a covered-dish dinner at one of our country churches where German influence is strong. While the food was being put on the table in the church basement, the men and boys stood outside in the sunshine. Mostly we talked about the crops and the weather. When everything was ready one of the ladies called us, and we trooped downstairs. We said grace. Then the women receded to the corners of the room or behind the table to serve, and the men and boys went through the line. After we had heaped our plates magnificently, and were seated and eating heartily, then the women got their food. Old arthritic grandmothers, mothers with babies, teen-age girls—all waited until we men were happily gorging ourselves before they began to eat. I was glad no woman's lib advocate was around. She would have had a fit. She would have blown that affair wide open. The funny thing was, the women were basking in their glory as the men gobbled up great quantities of food to the women's honor. Every bite said, "My compliments to the chef."

(Incidentally, the men still sit on one side of the church during worship; the women on the other. One young couple sits together. They're challenging the system.)

Another example took place on the college campus. At our liberal arts church college across the street, there were two kids who seemed very much in love. They had been dating for about two years. Both were conscientious, mature young adults. Aaron was Jewish, Sally was Methodist. They had so much in common—intelligence, school activities, personality factors. He even attended church with her. I was surpriesd when Aaron told me they had broken their engagement. "What happened?" I asked. "Well, she invited me to her home for dinner. Her family are great cooks—so is she. She was careful to fix foods that I could eat. But for dessert she served apple pie. It was delicious. Sally's mother commented that 'most women use shortening, but you can't beat *lard* for good old-fashioned pie crust.'" It never occurred to Sally or her mother that they were feeding Aaron pork, but it was obvious to Aaron. This fine young man, grandson of a rabbi, looked away from me, gazed across the Kansas prairies and said, "I decided that if something so insignificant as a tablespoon of lard could come between us, there was no use trying to make it work."

The third couple had a symbol that saved their marriage. It was work. Oh I know, nearly everybody works. But for John and Marie Rutherford, it was a compulsive symbol. It was an unlikely marriage. John was one of two children in an Anglo-Saxon Protestant family. They owned their own business, lived on the right side of the tracks. Marie's dad came from the old country, Italian Catholic. He was fifty when she was born. Marie was the tenth of eleven children. They were so poor that Marie started working when she was ten years old.

I remember clearly the day they came into my office for marriage counseling. Marie was expressive, emotive, volatile. John was quiet, tight-lipped, agreeable but detached. After fifteen years of marriage, they were ready to call it quits. Their level of communication was extremely poor. We put them in a small therapy group for several months, and exciting things happened to them. They really learned to talk and to laugh. One of my happiest pastoral memories was running into them in a restaurant one night. They were sitting alone at a table, hunched over, whispering to each other. As the story unraveled, John had been brought up under a Protestant work ethic. His mother and his father and his brother worked all the time. That is all they did. He met Marie at work. That was all she knew, too. After their marriage they worked together in their own store, day and night, seven days a week for fourteen years. They were both compulsive workers. They finally made enough money so that Marie did not need to work and John could take time off. Then, they did not know what to do with themselves. As a result of their group experiences and their newly fostered dialogue, they agreed to start up a new business from scratch and both work at it together again. Work was the strongest symbol they had, and they decided to hold onto it.

There are so many symbols. They are different in every home. One person's emotive symbol is another person's irrelevancy. You have some in your home; we have some in ours. For most people, *gifts* are significant nonverbal forms of communication. The jokes that commonly circulate about forgetting birthdays and anniversaries are like mother-in-law jokes. They are only half funny; part of the time they hurt.

Dr. Paul Tournier, Swiss psychiatrist and author, has written the most helpful book on *The Meaning of Gifts*[2] which has ever come to my attention. He makes it clear that all of us need to receive gifts. They are a form of reassurance. We all need to give gifts. It is a way of expressing love. But the gifts we give and the way we choose them, the ways we give and receive them—that's the rub. One man gave his wife a pipe each birthday and anniversary—for her collection. She did not smoke, but he did. One woman gave her husband a book, then spoiled it all by saying, "Hurry up and read it; I've been dying to read it myself." We gave our son Steve a microscope when he was four. I though it would be a great educational toy. As a gift, it was flop. A real gift says, "I know you. I know something about you. I know your size, your interest, your heart's desire." That's why gifts are so hard to give. To say "I love you" a gift needs to express something of the giver and to say something about the recipient. Ask yourself the question, what would *she/he really* like. It may be dumb, extravagant, frivolous, trivial. But the idea is to give something that will please, and with no strings attached.

Now, stop and think for a moment about some non-verbal behavior, some emotive symbols in *your marriage.* What are they? In your communicative system, what are some of the secret messages conveyed by smoke signals or sign language?

Here is one of ours. It's called "the vacuum cleaner episode." Julia is a pernickety housekeeper, especially when it comes to keeping things picked up. She doesn't leave mops or dustrags or clothes lying around. Even with our four rather rambunctious children, she has never permitted toys or games to be left scattered on the floor after the playing is over. It upsets her if I leave a sweater on a chair. In every parsonage where we have lived, we left behind a special set of pegs by the back door where each person learned to hang his coat. Without being fanatical about it, Julia simply runs an orderly house. But once in a while—say about every couple of months—a strange phenomenon takes place. I suddenly discover, right in the doorway to the bedroom, or smack in front of my chair at the table, or square in the middle of the living room, the vacuum cleaner. The cord is running in one direction; the hose is pointed in the other. It appears to the casual observer as if Julia were interrupted by a phone call or by some kettle boiling over in the kitchen. One might assume that the machine would soon be put back to work or else restored to its resting place in the closet. But it generally stays right were it is, like one of those broken-down covered wagons in Death Valley. And it stays there and stays there—sometimes for as long as two days and nights. Now you understand I have tried different approaches to the problem across the years. Sometimes I have gallantly stepped over the machine and back over it again, pleasantly pretending it did not exist and thinking that I was being quite charitable in not saying anything critical or derogatory. On other occasions I have caught it with a bare toe or tripped over it during the night or simply become tired of its ugliness. I have kicked it aside, exhorted it to go to a hotter climate, or yelled at my wife expressing hope that someday she would move the blankety blank thing. Now the interesting thing to me is that, on this issue, she never yells back. In fact, she never has said anything. The only time she has ever asked me to vacuum was when we were having a party, and she could not get everything done in time.

The truth is, the deserted vacuum cleaner is a kind of nonunion strike. It is a symbol that yells, *"I've had it.* I've had all the drudgery of keeping this house clean that I can take. My back hurts, and I wish to goodness that somebody would give me a hand." In one of my completely irrational moments the other day, I tried to evaluate where I thought she had already swept, and where she had not. I plugged in the sweeper and finished the room. I rolled up the cord and put it all away. I never said anything (if I had asked her where to sweep, she would have said that she would get to it after a while). When I finished she never said anything. But things seemed to go better. She was whistling and fixing lunch. Besides, I got the damned thing out of the way.

Food

When the whole marriage business was nicknamed bed and board, it was no accident. That is the name of the game. A house without a table or bed is no home. I have a friend whose name begins with S—we will call him Sully Sullivan. His wife has him all figured out. The other day she indicted him (and most husbands) when she said, "Sully has only four interests in the world, and they all begin with *s*." Then she enumerated them, slowly and carefully: *stomach, sex, sports,* and *Sully.* Then she added, *"And not always in that order!"*

Sex deserves a chapter of its own, but stomach is often in first place. It is amazing how important food symbols are to the average husband. Food can be fodder for communicating all sorts of things. Mealtime is an arena in which your role is acted out.

What is your concept of a good husband? What is your understanding of the role of a good wife? Chances are, these questions are answered most clearly around the dinner table. Is it the wife's responsibility to do the cooking? To set the table? To pour the coffee? In earlier societies the questions would never have been raised. In ours, the questions have as many answers as there are families. Is the husband supposed to help prepare the meals? Is he supposed to stay out of the kitchen—the "woman's domain"—until an "offering" can be placed before him. (In the oldest civilization, the Sumerians gave food offerings to the gods.) Much marital conflict today arises out of confused expectations about where we cook and where we eat.

Let me illustrate, I hope without too much prejudice, from our "board." As I have intimated, I grew up in a home that was rather traditional, midwestern and agricultural, with a strong dose of German "kraut" thrown in. My dad's middle name was Gustov; his mother's name was Knackstedt. We had potatoes twice a day. Mother loved to cook. She prepared the meals, set the table, and hurried back for extra goodies. She cleared the table, washed the dishes, and basked over any compliments which might be thrown her way. We used to say that Dad didn't know where the kitchen was.

Julia, on the other hand, grew up in a well-to-do southern home. A Negro woman served as cook and maid and lived in the home with them. Julia's mother loved to bring in fresh flowers for the table, supervise the menu, and sit at table like the southern lady she is. Julia's father either hired adequate help, or, in later years, helped to make a quick breakfast or wash the supper dishes. Julia would be the first to admit that she had never prepared a meal before we were married.

Talk about a mixed marriage!

Now the problem for us is: Who is supposed to fix the coffee each morning? According to my background, that's woman's work. No matter how many times the children have cried during the night, no matter how hard Julia had worked the day before, fixing the coffee is her responsibility. On those few occasions when I have magnanimously plugged in the percolator (after asking two or three times how much water, grounds, etc. were needed), I then proceeded to act as if I had just climbed Mount Everest. On the other hand, my wife has, under pressure of a growing family, my recalcitrance, and her own desires to be a good housewife, learned to make coffee most every morning. But, for a girl who grew up believing that women are ladies and ought to be treated as such, kitchen work is drudgery. If some morning I get up, make the coffee, and bring her a hot cup while she is waking up, she beams like a princess. When I do it (not often enough) I offer her a gift in which she sees respect, affection, and gratitude. I've noticed that one hot cup of coffee can make her happy for three days.

I don't know how it is in your marriage—what you expect and what your mate expects—but I know that the way you deal with food is a powerful part of your marital experience. Two observations: First, at the risk of making a lot of women angry, I have yet in my experience to meet a man who was critical because his wife treated him too well at the table. The modern American woman is educated, attractive, interested in many things, working in jobs of all descriptions, but she dare not forget the deep-seated yearnings of her husband to eat a good hot meal. It is a smart woman indeed who sees the table, not as a competition to her other interests, but as a part and parcel of her creative life. I think it was Samuel Johnson—who loved education and intellectual conversation—who nevertheless said, "A man is in general better pleased when he has a good dinner upon his table than when his wife talks Greek."

Second, the "times they are a-changin'." Times have changed since Grandmother canned applesauce and put up her own mincemeat. She made her own knackwurst and blutwurst, and soaked her own kraut. (We remember with nostalgia the rows of pretty jars on the pantry shelf and the smells coming from the wood-burning stove, but we forget the varicose veins, the fallen uteruses, and the fat, starchy diets.) Though there is some hunger for the primitive among the youth—and folks in mental hospitals are learning again to work with their hands—still, *the old days are gone*. The modern American woman is a million light years removed from that style of life.

Recent government statistics indicate that one half of all women of working age are currently employed outside the home. Women are factory workers, clerks, salesgirls, business and professional people. It is now the predominant style of life. So what does that have to say about the old coffeepot, the homemade bread, and fresh apple pie? Well, it means that we are forced to redefine some role expectations. It means some of the old expressions like, "The woman's place is in the home," just will not carry the mail anymore. Couples living in communes designate duties to different persons according to their time and abilities. More and more we are doing that in our normal homes. For many people, schedules are weird and responsibilities are varied. A registered nurse, who works from 3:00 p.m. until 11:00 p.m. in the emergency room, is not going to fix a candlelight supper for her husband each evening. She may be smart enough to fix one on her day off sometimes, but most of the time, hubby is going to have to pick up the slack. Two young married kids, trying to make it through junior college, may have to alternate as to who will make the peanut butter and jelly sandwiches tonight.

Some things, however, are still emotionally valid, and they always will be. The breaking of bread is sacramental. Deep within us are formative feelings generated at our mother's breast. A baby learns to suck, to feel good, to trust, and to love. Rueul Howe suggests that the way a mother feeds her child contributes to the love he will find at the Communion table.[3] Meals where people laugh, and talk, and enjoy themselves are a kind of mini-communion. It is a wise husband who helps fill in the gaps, throws old styles out the window, and learns to enjoy sharing the kitchen.

And, aw shucks, I still hope Julia will make a fresh apple pie for us this weekend.

Sex Is God's Idea

Hung-Up on Sex

In spite of billboard bosoms and Madison Avenue pornography, we are a sex-starved society. It is a strange paradox: on the surface we are sex-saturated; deep down we are sexually inhibited. Our obsession with X-rated movies and lewd paperbacks only shows the poverty of our sexual experiences.

As a people, we are a lot like Marilyn Monroe. The onetime sex goddess was married to Joe Dimaggio, Arthur Miller, et al. She was showered with adulation by millions of virile American men. But she wrote in her suicide note: "I need somebody to love me." Our problem is not too much sex; it is too little sex. Oh, we have plenty of superficial, secondhand, back-seat sex. We have too much stag movie, lonely soldier, switch-wives sex. But we are desperately short of deep, soul-level, sacramental sex—the kind the Creator had in mind.

The church is partly to blame. We have spent most of our time and energy saying no-no; we have put precious little emphasis on yes-yes. In Protestant circles we have been a thousand times more concerned about whether Susie got pregnant before her marriage than we have been with whether Susie had sexual joy and fulfillment after her marriage. Catholics, stressing procreation on one hand and celibacy on the other, have often forgotten to extol the significance of sexual satisfaction.

Actually, sex is God's idea. Some people seem to think that it is the invention of a Hollywood promoter. The Bible, however, says it all so clearly. "So God created man in his own image . . . male and female he created them. And God blessed them, and God said to them, 'Be fruitful and multiply. . . . And God saw everything he had made, and behold it was very good" (Gen. 1:27-28, 31—Augustine translated the verse: "Behold it was *very, very* good"). In another biblical account "God said, 'It is not good that the man should be alone; I will make a helper fit for him.' . . . So the Lord God caused a deep sleep to fall upon the man, and while he slept took one of his ribs and closed up its place with flesh, and the rib which the Lord God had taken from the man he made into a woman and brought her to the man. . . . 'This at last is bone of my bones and flesh of my flesh; she shall be called Woman because she was taken out of Man" (Gen. 2:18, 21-23).

One of the ancient rabbis, in explaining the poetry of the rib story, put it in these beautiful words: "God made Eve out of Adam's rib so that she would be beneath his arm for him to protect her, close to his heart for him to love her, and at his side to walk in full equality with her. In the wisdom of God he did not take a bone from Adam's hand lest Adam use her as a tool. He did not take a bone from Adam's foot lest he tread upon her. He did not take a bone from Adam's head lest she try to dominate him. But out of his side a rib was taken that together they might be partners side by side for life."[1]

The the creation story, to nail it down, says: "And the man and his wife were both naked, and were not ashamed" (Gen. 2:25). Sex was not the forbidden fruit. The snake does not have any Freudian implications. God meant for Adam and Eve to enjoy complete connubial bliss under the fruit trees in the garden. They were one flesh. Only when they became proud and disobedient did their sex life get all fouled up. Only then did they feel shame. Only then did they hide their nakedness from God. "She took of its fruit and ate; and she also gave some to her husband, and he ate. Then the eyes of both were opened, and they knew that they were naked; and they sewed fig leaves together and made themselves aprons" (Gen. 3:6b-7).

The Reverend Malcomb Boyd reports that an active churchman once said to him, "When I am engaged with my wife in the sexual act, God turns his back." Father Boyd claims that he told the man that was an awful thing to say about God, about sex, and about his wife. Well, those are strong words, but the point is well made. The marriage bed is God's gift, God's plan, God's design. The Father in his infinite wisdom created sexuality for mankind in order to provide the intimacy of companionship for a man and his wife and to extend his divine creativity into the realm of human participation.

What a pity we have lost some of the Jewish rootage to our Christian faith. The old Hebrews could never have understood all of our hang-ups about sexuality (the hang-ups come from classical Greek philosophy). For the ancient Jews, it was normal and wholesome for a man and his wife to enjoy their sexual relations. They had no weird Protestant guilt feelings over experiencing pleasure, no corrupted Catholic concepts about purity being nonsexual. Tucked away in the wisdom of Ecclesiastes are these delightful words: "If two lie together, they are warm; but how can one be warm alone?" (4:11). "Let your garments be always white; let not oil be lacking on your head. Enjoy life with the wife whom you love, all the days of your vain life which he has given you under the sun" (9:8-9). And I have always wondered why nobody ever bothers to read the Song of Solomon—the loveliest, sexiest, innocently pure book in the Bible!

How graceful are your feet in sandals,
   O queenly maiden!
Your rounded thighs are like jewels,
   the work of master hand.
Your navel is a rounded bowl
   that never lacks mixed wine. . . .
Your two breasts are like two fawns,
   twins of a gazelle.
How fair and pleasant you are,
   O loved one, delectable maiden!
You are stately as a palm tree,
   and your breasts are like its clusters.
I say I will climb the palm tree
   and lay hold of its branches.
Oh, may your breasts be like clusters of the vine,
   and the scent of your breath like apples,
And your kisses like the best wine
   that goes down smoothly,
   sliding over lips and teeth.
                    (Song of Solomon 7:1-3, 6-9)

Even a tough, grisly old bachelor like the apostle Paul understood the sexuality of marriage. Paul has really been given a bad press. Listen to this:

The husband should give to his wife her conjugal rights, and likewise the wife to her husband. For the wife does not rule over her own body, but the husband does; likewise the husband does not rule over his own body, but the wife does. Do not refuse one another except perhaps by agreement for a season that you may devote yourselves to prayer; but then come together again, lest Satan tempt you through lack of self-control. (I Cor. 7:3-5)

Imagine! Paul says not to refuse one another except by common agreement—and then only for a period of prayer. He even suggests that the prayer time ought not to be too long.

One of the satisfactions of helping men and women find a fresh experience with God is that it often frees them sexually. A religion of rules often inhibits and frustrates. A faith founded on an encounter with divine love releases wellsprings of sexuality within a marriage. I heard recently the delightful testimony of a man who had been floundering toward divorce. He and his wife had tried all kinds of medicine, counseling, and resolutions. Finally one night they knelt together beside their bed, surrendered themselves to God's love in Christ, and felt his love flow into them. In laughter and tears, they crawled into bed, locked in each others arms, yielded to an unconditional love. Today they actually date their marriage from that holy night.

When Jesus was questioned about marriage and divorce, he grounded his answer in the act of creation. "In the beginning, at the creation, [that is, from the first impulses of God's creative activity] God made them male and female. For this cause shall a man leave his father and mother, and be made one with his wife; and the two shall become one flesh. It follows that they are no longer two individuals: they are one flesh" (Mark 10:6-8, NEB). The sexual implications were no accident. The sexual act symbolizes and actualizes the oneness of marital union.

It is interesting to think that when Paul wanted to compare the spiritual joy of the unity between Christ and his people, he could find no higher analogy than that of the union between bride and bridegroom. And there was no spiritualizing of it either. The physical realities are clearly in Paul's mind:

Wives, be subject to your husbands, as to the Lord. . . . Husbands, love your wives, as Christ loved the church and gave himself up for her. . . . Husbands should love their wives as their own bodies. . . . This is a great mystery, and I take it to mean Christ and his church. (Eph. 5:22, 25, 28, 32)

To tell you the truth, I think that the more powerful sex becomes, the more spiritual it is. Or, to say it another way, the more sex is related to the love of God, the more meaningful and exciting—and fun—it is. I have a friend, a doctor named Norman Harris, who is a gynecologist and obstetrician. He claims that sex is 90 percent from the neck up. Not one to overlook the physical, Dr. Harris simply realizes that what flows out of the heart—kindness or meanness, understanding or selfishness, patience or rudeness—is what makes it beautiful or ugly. That is why so much so-called sex education simply misses the mark. What we need primarily is not a lesson in physiology, but the power to relate deeply in loyal love to another person.

Marriage Is for Sex

I do not know about you, but I was raised thinking that sex is *permissable* in marriage. Isn't that a weak, milk-toast concept? Where in the world did we get the idea that sex is exciting only if it is sneaky—like a boy smoking a cigar behind the barn? Who put out the notion that sex in marriage is dull, routine, and ordinary? I suppose that we listen to the wrong people. We read what some neurotic actor who has been married five times has to say about love and marriage. Or we listen to the divorcée at the beauty shop who knows all the answers but has never made them work. Do you read the movie and the "true love" magazines? You would think that the jet set really knows the score. Maybe part of the problem is that the people who understand the joys and satisfactions of true sexual intimacy and secure marital relationships do not say a lot about it. Maybe they are like deep rivers that carry most of the freight but do not make the gurgles and splashes of the flood creeks and mountain streams.

When I talk to couples who are planning to get married, I tell them that God wants them to have fun in their bed. As long as any activity is mutually satisfying, there are literally no holds barred. No religious

scruples, no church laws, no social legislation prohibits
what a husband and wife can say or do in the privacy of
their bedroom, as long as they bring pleasure to each
other. Naturally, anything which hurts or degrades or
offends is unacceptable. But enthusiasm, by man and
woman, in showing love can be unbridled. "Against
such there is no law" (Gal. 5:23b).

Dr. Karl Menninger makes a great case for marriage
providing the environs for rich sexual expression. In
his book, *Love Against Hate,* he writes:

> In the light of modern psychoanalytic theory, living and
> loving are almost synonymous; one may say that eating
> one's food and kissing one's bride are merely differently
> directed expressions of the same drive. Marriage is a com-
> promise, molded legally, economically and religiously for
> providing a dependable opportunity for the expression of
> the erotic life.

Dr. Menninger continues:

> The unfortunate thing is that in conventional thinking the
> sexual life per se is accorded only a low degree of respect.
> It continues to be regarded by many if not most people as
> something of a necessary evil, *permitted* only under cer-
> tain carefully supervised conditions.
> For, conditioned as they are by their childhood experi-
> ences, men and women in contemporary civilization grow
> up *ill prepared to reap the full benefits of the erotic oppor-
> tunity provided in marriage.*[2]

People who are trying to maximize love through casual encounters are simply missing the boat. Young
people who hope to authenticate sex by tentative co-
habitation have been fed false data about erotic pleasure. Someone needs to tell them "plain out" that there
is deep joy in knowing that the woman who kissed you
passionately in the night is going to sing softly while
she fixes you eggs for breakfast. She is the same woman
who will carry your babies and rock your grandbabies.

Sex needs security in order to blossom. If I had to wonder who my sexual partner would be this week (the way I wondered as a teen-ager whom I would take to the dance on Saturday) I would go out of my mind. It has taken my wife nearly twenty years to get some messages across to me. And she still has a lot to say. Come to think of it, so do I.

Women are sexual too. But a lot of gals have been taught otherwise. Some think they are supposed to be passive. Others do not know that anything exciting is supposed to happen. It is not unusual for a woman to come into a pastor's study or a counselor's office complaining about being nervous and high strung. Chances are she is skinny and chain smoking. She may have three children, but sexual fulfillment—sexual climax—has escaped her. That is the kind of situation the psychological sex clinics love to exploit. Unfortunately, that kind of frustration is not rare. Dr. Menninger claims that most American women are sexually frustrated. He says that there is a myth abroad in the land that portrays the "male as a sexual beast and the female as a frigid madonna." He claims this is the result of "vicious, hypocritical residuum from Pauline and Victorian ethics."[3] Now I don't find frigid madonnas in Paul's writing, but I do find them in the pastor's study.

Anyway, our job is not to cast the blame, it is to find the answer. It is time that we recognized that erotic pleasure is both good and necessary. A whole revolution would occur if wives and husbands began trying to provide the greatest possible erotic enjoyment for their mates. Why not? That is what marriage is for. If husbands knew half as much about their wives' feelings as they do their cars' motors, their marriages would run a whole lot better. Because sex is so highly personal, the so-called sex books are not a lot of help either. Does she like to be kissed on the ear? Maybe. Maybe not. Is a good back-rub with lotion relaxing? Or does it put her to sleep? Does she enjoy having her breasts caressed?

When? For some women deep kissing is exciting; for others it is disgusting. A husband has to be patient enough, and smart enough, to figure all this out. So does the wife. And it is not the same every time. Sometimes he has to ask if that feels good. Sometimes she has to tell him. How else are two people ever to find out?

Speed for men is a common problem. Let the wife give reassurance by word and action that the guy does not have to hurry to prove his manhood. It is a game; lets play it, and play it so that everybody wins! I still find in counseling, tragic ignorance of the woman's clitoris. That small "woman's penis," slightly above the vagina, is the sensitive, critical area. A gentle massaging of the clitoris by fingers, lips, or penis normally arouses the woman toward climax. A wife, by using her hands, can touch her husband's genitals, so that he decides, "why hurry." Unfortunately, unbelievable numbers of couples fail to take the time to really enjoy each other. They muddle their communications so that the fun and satisfaction are lost. The husband lacks the joy of having deeply satisfied his wife so he is emotionally frustrated. The wife is physically unsatisfied and subconsciously angry.

The great thing about marriage is that there is time for experimentation and for trying again. Some couples find pleasure in their love-making after ten or fifteen years of confusion and trying. Sometimes it is not so funny. But sometimes it is. We ought to laugh more than we do—we take it too seriously. I was recently delighted to read an article in *Marriage Magazine* which gaily advocated sex before breakfast. I wish I had read it twenty years ago.

In our homes we ought to be nurturing our children to enjoy the touch, to take pleasure in hugs and kisses, to feel comfortable in mother's lap or holding daddy's hand. The psychologist Erik Erikson says that we learn to trust people in our early years through touch. Little children need to be permitted to play. Some of our happiest memories are times our kids played and splashed together in the bathtub. A lot of freedom to play sexually is formed in early childhood. According to Dr. Vernard Eller, sexual foreplay really begins when a person is a baby in bed with his mother. The nursing and cuddling and bouncing are just the beginnings of a whole life of play in which a growing child learns to enjoy other people.[4] Babies who did not learn to trust through touch grow up into men and women who are afraid of warmth and affection and sexual play. But exciting things can still be learned. Take it from a highly structured, work-oriented puritan like myself—or take it from a no-no-oriented, nice girl like my wife—a couple can still learn to have a ball together if they try.

Sex Is for Marriage

How does a preacher say it? Without pulling out moral codes or religious admonitions, how can a pastor who has heard the cries of agony from guilt-ridden people explain the tragic effects of premarital and extramarital sex? We could quote the Bible about the sins of fornication and adultery. Or we could quote psychiatrists like Dr. Max Levin of the New York Medical College who claims that the woman particularly is injured emotionally by sex before marriage.

The unmarried daughter today is beguiled by the rosy promises of a "new era." She is told that moral standards belong to the past, and that the watchword today is "freedom." She goes off to college with a sense of excitement. She will now live it up. There will be gay football weekends, with wild parties at the fraternity houses, followed by parties for just two at the motel. But she is not shown the small print in the contract. She is told nothing of the cost of sexual freedom, of its threat to her emotional well being. The young unmarried woman sells herself short when she gives herself to a man whose primary goal is to exploit her. She diminishes herself in her own eyes as well as his.[5]

But all this still sounds terribly like "preacher talk." Nobody wants to listen to that.

A year ago I was invited to meet with groups of high school seniors to talk about courtship and marriage. School was out for the entire day. In one group a girl got things rolling fast. "What's so magic about twenty minutes in front of the altar? I mean, everything is supposed to be naughty before the wedding, and then, presto, it's OK. How come? What's wrong with sex if you really love each other?"

I sat back and thought, while some of the kids gave the pat answers she was expecting from me.

"The Bible says it's a sin," one girl replied.

"You might get pregnant," one boy commented.

"Yeah, or get caught by your folks," said another.

Then there was silence. It was obvious that the questioner was not satisfied with the answers. So I decided to push things further. "Suppose you didn't get caught," I said. "Suppose you didn't get pregnant or become infected with a venereal disease or anything like that, then what would be wrong?" One young lady who was already engaged answered thoughtfully, "Your relationship might break up before you were married, and then you would feel bad. You would feel hurt. You would have shared a secret experience, kind of promised each other things, and then, if you broke up, you would feel blue and lonely. You would feel sort of secondhand if you fell in love again." (While she was talking, my thoughts raced back to a teen-aged girl who had been sleeping with her fiancé. When the engagement broke up, she slipped into the church late one night, and unbeknown to me, sat in my office all night crying. She required several months of counseling before she could look the world in the eye again.)

A boy piped up: "I've heard a lot of people say that you need to know whether you're compatible before you get married." Then he laughed, and as an aside to a buddy commented, "You have to try the shoes on before you buy them." That seemed to make sense to some, so I asked, "What are the conditions under which most premarital sex takes place?" Several of the girls saw the light immediately:

"You'd be afraid."

"You'd be in a hurry."

"If you were in a car or a motel or something, it wouldn't be like being in your own home."

But they still didn't understand what sex is supposed to be. So I tried another tack. "Sex is a deep language, deeper than words. The German poet Goethe said 'The highest cannot be spoken.' Now what do you think sex is trying to say?"

Of course someone said, "It means I love you."

"But what does that mean?" I probed. Finally they began to explore the thought.

"It means I belong to you."

"It means we will look after each other."

"It means I am giving myself completely to you."

"It means I am going to take care of you."

Now they were on target. I told them a true story. Once I had a fullback from the university football team come into my office to talk about marrying a girl in our church. He seemed a little casual. So I simply asked, "Are you ready to accept responsibility for this young lady's physical, emotional, financial, and spiritual well-being for the rest of her life?" His face blanched. His voice got high. "Is that what I'm getting ready to do?" It was fun to talk with him during the next several months. He carefully worked through that question. He explored the implications. When he finally said, "I do," he said it loud and clear.

Somehow we've got to avoid teaching our youth that sex is dirty or naughty or ugly—in a cheap parental effort to slow down the flow of vital adolescent juices. That makes for frozen marriages. That creates men and women—women especially—who have padlocked the door so tight that they cannot unlock it even in marriage. It is high time we lifted sex to a level of beauty and loveliness, so that—like all precious things—it can be restricted to say and do special things. It is like the Holy Sacrament. It needs to be guarded carefully. But then, under the proper conditions, it is to be experienced over and over to enrich our lives.

Our small group of seniors was about to wind up the discussion. Our time was nearly over. With a couple of minutes left, I asked if anyone in the group had a clear conviction of what sex meant to him. A beautiful blond girl—actually an eighteen-year-old woman—spoke for the first time. She was what the kids would call "real cool." With carefully chosen words, she said, "When we date, we start giving gifts. At first the gifts are fairly impersonal—like flowers or a box of candy. But as we become closer, our gifts become more personal, more intimate. When kids go steady they give matched sweaters or class rings. When a man and a woman are engaged, they give very special things—a diamond and very personal things for Christmas. The most personal gift that I can ever give is myself. I have nothing more precious to give. When I marry I want to give my husband the best that I have. I want to give him my whole self as completely as I can."

We sat in silence for a few seconds until the bell rang. Nobody had anything else to say.

6

In This Corner We Have...

The Importance of Fighting

Do you and your spouse fight? No? Tell the truth. Just a little spat now and then? Sometimes a pretty good argument? Aha, yes. On occasion, you have a good old-fashioned, knock-down-drag-out, honest-to-goodness, scream-so-the-neighbors-can-hear, slam-the-door, burst-into-tears, pout-all-day kind of fight? Well, join the human race. That's where most of us live.

Where did we get the idea that men and women with good marriages do not fight? Maybe we got the notion that anger is bad from the same place we learned that sex is dirty. Hostility is essential to human personality. Expressed anger—fighting—is normative in a good marriage. Psychologists differ about the source of aggression. Some say it is one of the basic drives; others argue that it represents the frustration of the basic drive. But aggression is there, nonetheless, and it is essential to life. Without hostility a man would never plow a field, cut down a tree, write a book, or love a woman. Without energizing hostility, a woman would never sew a seam, teach a class, give a hypo, or deliver a baby.

So it is only natural that there should be conflict in marriage. (Wouldn't it be boring otherwise? Of course, a little boredom, like a short vacation, is nice *once* in a while.) Julia and I sang a song in a corny program once.

83

It went like this: "Friendship, friendship, what a beautiful blendship!" But marriage is not a "blendship"—not two souls merging into a common vapor. It's more like a team of horses, usually pulling together, but occasionally geeing and hawing. Nobody wants to be swallowed up. Everybody needs to be a person in his own right. That means tension, at least in this world.

Most couples hide their fights. Sophisticated folks use words rather than pots and pans. The words hurt more. We try not to let the neighbors know. Some people do not fight in front of the kids, as if kids cannot sense tension or sniff out an emotional lie. Anger is considered "not nice" in spite of the fact that Jesus, in his perfect humanness, chastised Peter, cursed the fig tree, and drove the money changers from the temple. Most couples will admit only to "differences" or "silly little arguments."

I have visited homes where they yelled at the kids, where husband and wife tangled once in a while, where you knew there was an occasional eruption of volcanic proportions. For the most part, they were alive, vibrant homes. But have you ever walked into a house where the silence was so thick you could cut it with a knife? I have. I thought I was walking down death row at Sing Sing. Do you remember the old man who claimed that he and his wife hadn't had a cross word in over twenty years. Come to find out, in all that time they *hadn't spoken at all.*

Fighting in marriage is a vital form of communication. There's no way to get along without it. Of course, there are ways to civilize it, make it creative, and lessen its severity. But true intimacy is simply not possible without expressed hostility. Hostility cannot be healthy without conflict—tugging, testing, struggling, fighting. Even sex, our most intimate symbol of dialogue, clearly contains hostile responses in the very moment of passion—the bite on the ear, the fingernail in the back, the hurting squeeze.

Bad Fights

If all fights were good, however, it would be a different world. Conflict can turn into war. People get mangled, maimed, and killed. Most of the murders that are committed in America are domestic affairs. Words can detroy a personality. Conflict can tear a relationship to shreds like a tiger tearing a piece of meat. Any argument that undermines a person's self-confidence is a seriously bad fight.

George Bach and Peter Wyden, in their best seller, *The Intimate Enemy* describe countless ways of bad fighting.[1] Here are a few tragic mistakes that you might watch out for the next time things break loose at your house:

"Gunny sacking." Some people pick up irritations, one by one, and do not say anything. They gather grievances, disappointments, and hurts and put them in the "gunny sack." They "tote" this growing burden around until it finally breaks open. Somebody says "boo," and all sorts of pent-up feelings burst out—much to the surprise of everybody.

"Generalizing." When we start fighting dirty, we begin to say things like "you never" or "you always." *One* time you lay your coat on the kitchen table and she says: "You *never* hang up *anything!* You never will learn to put things away. I'll bet your father didn't hang up his clothes either. Men are all alike—slobs." What could have been a minor quarrel over your failure to hang up your coat in a particular instance now turns into a minor war. You naturally feel wronged because *sometimes* you have hung up *some things.* Another way to generalize is to use labels. Or you could term it "name-calling." Call somebody a "sex maniac." Or say, "I think you're mentally ill." That will make him angry, because nobody can tolerate being depersonalized into a category.

"Contaminating the sheets." Why fight in the bedroom all the time? Don't spoil the atmosphere there, especially if the fight has nothing to do with sleeping or sex. Julia and I used to go to bed and start talking about how we should be disciplining the children. Since we were tired, we often developed an argument that had nothing to do with the bedroom. Dr. Bach says that a couple ought to get out of bed, go into the living room, and have it out. Then when they kiss and make up, they've got someplace else to go.

"Throwing the kitchen sink." You know the old expression, "He threw everything but the kitchen sink." Well, in some arguments, people look for everything they can conceivably think of, including the "kitchen sink." They throw that too. Julia calls it throwing antiques. Every quarrel of the past is dredged up and thrown into the fray. The time Mother said she thought you could keep a cleaner house, the year he forgot your anniversary, the night he got loaded and made eyes at that sexy blond—everything is tossed into the contemporary argument. I remember a water fight I once had in a cow pond. My buddy and I started out having a lot of fun—splashing water on a hot July day. Soon though, we were reaching into the bottom of the pond and throwing handfuls of mud and manure. The fight really got "dirty."

Dr. Bach quotes this exchange which illustrates the kitchen-sink syndrome:

He: Why were you late?

She: I tried my best.

He: Yeah? You and who else? Your mother is never on time either.

She: That's got nothing to do with it.

He: The hell it doesn't. You're just as sloppy as she is.

She: *(getting louder)*: You don't say! Who's picking whose dirty underwear off the floor every morning?

He: *(sarcastic but controlled)*: I happen to go to work. What have *you* got to do all day?

She: *(shouting)*: I'm trying to get along on the money you don't make, that's what.

He: *(turning away from her)*: Why should I knock myself out for an ungrateful bitch like you?[2]

If you reach back into the garbage of the centuries every time you quarrel, you're going to have a lot of bad scenes.

"Hitting below the belt." Everyone has points of extreme vulnerability. It may be a nickname. It may be a facial feature. One wise man advised couples never to point in derision to something the other could not possibly change. A man or woman who is trying to live down a shameful experience of the past such as a jail sentence or a baby born out of wedlock, is likely to be injured by having that thrown up during an argument. That is hitting below the belt. A person has the right to yell foul. That is like putting a horseshoe in the boxing gloves. In twisted, ugly marriages this rule is not understood. A referee is needed. That's why a counselor or therapy group can help. They can provide an arena where someone can yell foul if the fighting is unfair.

Judith Viorst, in a delightful poem, shows that she knows something about fighting. She also shows a sense of humor, and that has saved many a marriage. In "Striking Back" she lists her own ways of "fighting dirty."

> When a husband tells a wife
> Stop screaming at the children
> And he isn't crazy about the drapes
> And why doesn't she learn where Thailand is
> And maybe she should cut her hair
> (All of which, needless to say, are implicit attacks on her
> Intelligence,
> Taste,
> Desirability,
> And maternal instincts)

A wife
Can only
Strike back.

So sometimes I try
My mother's technique
Which is silence for a week,
A brooding stare into the ruined future,
And no rouge for that look of
You are making me so miserable you are giving me
A fatal illness.

It occasionally works.

And sometimes I try
Weeping, cursing, expressions of bitter remorse,
And don't ever expect to see the children again,
Which I often follow with phone calls pricing suites
At expensive hotels.

I've had limited success.

There is also
The psychoanalytic confrontation
Which entails informing him
(More, of course, in sorrow than in anger)
That his sadistic treatment of those who love him is a
     sign of unconscious feelings of inadequacy and
He needs help.

I've dropped this approach.

But there is always
Total recall
During which all the wrongs he has done me since
    first we met
Are laid before him.
And when this is combined
With refusing to go to the Greenberg's annual
    costume party,
Tossing and moaning in my sleep,

And threatening to commit suicide, take a lover,
and drop out of the PTA because why try to
save the school system when my entire uni-
verse is falling apart.
I start to feel
I'm really
Striking back.[3]

Games People Play

Ever since Dr. Eric Berne wrote his popular book,
Games People Play,[4] the notion of emotional game-
playing has become a part of our everyday vocabulary.
My eighth-grade son, Paul, has just formed a musical
group (would you believe "The Bachelor Six"?). One of
the pop songs they play is a takeoff on Dr. Berne's book.
It helps us laugh at ourselves, our masks, our hypoc-
risies. With a rock beat they sing, "Oh the games people
play now," and chide us for our human masquerade.

We necessarily pattern a lot of our behavior, but unfortunately, some of these patterns are destructive. What
Berne calls games are predictable patterns, basically dis-
honest interrelationships, which, while involving dramatic contesting, *actually avoid conflict*.

Here is one. Berne calls it, "If It Wern't for You."
Most of us chose a mate who meets some of our needs.
If we are weak in a given area, we often marry someone who has that strength. Now, this game begins when
we accuse our mate of *causing* our weakness. A shy
timid woman, for instance, married a forceful extrovert
husband. At parties, she hides in the corner while he
circulates, swapping stories with the men. She decides
that her weakness is his fault. She blames him for taking her to parties where the people aren't any fun. She
blames him for monopolizing the conversation. She
says, "If it weren't for you I would have finished college—then I could converse with intelligent people."
She cries, "If it weren't for you I would associate with
friends I felt comfortable with." She may even become

frigid, claiming, "If it weren't for you I would be warm and outgoing." This pattern is not true conflict. It is actually a copping-out from responsibility. Allowed to continue, it will destroy their home. A therapist, or an extremely wise husband has to stop this game by letting her weakness rear its ugly head. That means giving her complete freedom until she admits she is frightened. "Honey, if you want to go to the university in the evening, I'll stay home with the kids." Or, "You decide what friends you want to be with, and that is where we'll go." When her weakness is unmasked, then it can be dealt with openly.

Another sad game is called "Corner." In this encounter, one or both persons get "painted into a corner." Nobody can move. Usually one makes a threat, and it is taken literally by the other. A lot of divorces come about by cornered people.

It is the night of the big club dance. Twenty-five dollar tickets are bought and paid for. Both Mr. and Mrs. B. are dressing:

Mrs. B.:   Look at these shoes. They look terrible.
Mr. B.:   Good Lord, you've bought a new dress. Don't tell me you need new shoes. This dance is costing me a fortune.
Mrs. B: I'm embarrassed to go, looking like this.
Mr. B.:   Now I suppose you're going to back out.
Mrs. B.:   I'm not going in these shoes.
Mr. B.:   Hell, why don't you stay home and I'll just go by myself.
Mrs. B.:   Go ahead and go. See if I care.

Mrs. B. rips off her dress, and Mr. B. stomps out of the house. Both are disappointed and confused. Neither quite understands how they got painted in a corner. A beautiful evening was ruined. The event could have been so easily salvaged if Mr. B. had recognized an outcropping of insecurity and the need for reassurance. Mrs. B. could have ignored his threat, knowing that really was not what he meant to have happen. Of course, even at the end, Mr. B. could have laboriously tried to sweeten her up, but it is hard at that point, especially if, subconsciously, his wife was a little frightened by the affair. It turned out to be a kind of game that lacked true confrontation.

A fight behavior which is technically not a game is what I call a *pattern behavior*. We slip into fight ruts. Somebody touches the same sore spot; we respond in the usual way. The routine is on. It's like playing an old familiar record—you even know where the scratches are. Lately Julia has been breaking up these patterns. If something starts bubbling, if it looks as if we are going down familiar trails, she will suddenly say, "Hey, aren't we playing the old song again?" Sure enough, after twenty years of marriage, some trails are not worth walking down again; all the grass has been trampled. If she does not put the salt and pepper on the table at supper, well, there is not much point in griping. I know how it is going to turn out, so why spoil supper. There are a lot more important things to talk about, so why play the record again.

But the worst form of fighting is when somebody withdraws and will not fight at all. Like all forms of dialogue, "it takes two to tango." Both have to have the courage to make themselves vulnerable. Dialogue has to be mutual and must proceed from both sides.

I know lots of people, and so do you, who say, "It takes two to have a fight and I won't fight." Usually they say it with a kind of self-righteous smugness, as if they were saints or something. Dr. Bach calls them "doves." Doves in marriage can be deadly. The nonfighter is likely to be the most vicious fighter of all. If Silent Sam is married to Hurricane Helen, what happens? Hurricane Helen rants and raves—desperately trying to get some rise out of him—but old Sam just smiles like a chessy cat and goes on about his business. Or he clamps down on his cigar and stomps out of the house. He goes down to the corner bar and leaves H. Helen climbing the walls. There are many ways to withdraw. Some disappear. Some drink. Some go to their rooms and cry. But they are great manipulators and terrible communicators. Actually the dove is afraid to get into the arena and mix it up. He is afraid of getting hurt, or else he is afraid of hurting someone else.

Good Fights

Just as boxers need to have an arena in which to box, so marital fights need to be bounded by certain disciplines. Just as there are rules in an athletic contest, so there are rules for interesting, creative, productive fighting. Good partners fight with each other like two tennis players. They play within the rules and do not need a referee. In twisted, ugly marriages either they do not know the rules, or else refuse to fight by them, and they need a referee. Dr. Bach teaches couples in his group work how to fight fair in love and marriage.

Here are some disciplines to practice in your home:

a) *Deal with issues promptly.* Learn to level with one another quickly. We don't do this with casual acquaintances, but with intimate family or friends, it is essential. If there is transparency in normal, everyday communication, then leveling is natural. Of course, there are times and places when it is inappropriate to fight. It is an ugly scene to watch a couple fighting in the grocery store or at the bridge party. That brings additional embarrassment and shame. It is better to walk down a shady lane or go someplace and park. But the conflict needs to be done quickly. Actually the New Testament supports this concept of prompt attention to anger. Paul urged Christians not to "let the sun go down on your anger" (Eph. 4:26). That's good. It does not deny anger, but wants it to be dealt with promptly. It is a great marriage where the air is cleared each night and where sleep is approached in love and trust. Jesus supported this strategy of promptness with his teaching on reconciliation with a brother. If you bring a gift to the altar, and remember that you have offended your brother (it could be your wife) go immediately and make it right. Then come and offer your gift (Matt. 5:23-24). Long delays are bad. They lead to "gunny sacking," distorted dialogue, and repressed rage.

b) *Stick to the issues.* If we are arguing over a particular problem, let's hold it to that. It is difficult to play tennis, basketball, and football all at the same time. Besides, we tend to kitchen-sink if we don't. In a good fight, someone will say, "Hey, I've got a bone to pick with you." The other will answer, "OK, what is it?"

"You tracked mud in all over my fresh cleaned carpet."
"I cleaned my feet outdoors."
"You didn't clean them enough."
"Let's go look. You're so darn meticulous."
"See, mud all over."
"A little bit, I see. You're making a mountain out of a mud pie. If we had a throw rug out front, this wouldn't happen. Here, give me that sweeper and get us a new door mat so I don't have to take off my shoes every time it rains."

Now if the conflict progresses properly, they will have somehow cleaned up the mess, they will have worked through the tension, and they may even improve the entrance to the house.

c) *Fight it through.* Remember the goal is not for someone to win and someone to lose. The goal is to work through a problem without either person being destroyed. No one must have his ego strength diminished. Self-confidence, self-image must not be undermined. Threats are bad. If someone calls a bluff, it can be a standoff. Withdrawal ruins the possibilities of working it through. If Momma goes to the bedroom, locks the door and weeps, it is hard for the fight to continue to a satisfactory conclusion. We need to stay with it until it is worked through or until we are both exhausted. We only have about an hour's adrenalin in our fight energy, so we eventually run down emotionally. After that, we need to try to make up.

Lately I've been using an expression that has been fun. With someone close, with whom I don't see eye to eye, I say: "I'm going to put one corner of a handkerchief in my teeth and you're going to put a corner in your teeth, and we're going to settle this issue." It is only a figure of speech, but it creates a proper mood for conflict. Everybody knows the score, and we get to the bottom of the affair without hard feelings.

But in most husband-wife quarrels, there are lots of hurt feelings. There are some wounds after every fight. Making-up is the only satisfactory conclusion to a fight. The secret is to end up somehow by saying, "I love you." That is really what the fight was about anyway. If I can say "Honey, I love you," she might respond, "You know I didn't mean all those things I said, I love you too." That is the good and proper conclusion of a fight. Sexual intercourse can conclude a good fight beautifully. Those who say, "How could I possibly make love after all those cross words?" are either playing games (using the fight as an excuse) or else they have not worked the fight to its conclusion.

Goal of a Good Fight

The purpose of a fight is not to maim, hurt, or destroy your mate. Rather it is to communicate honest feelings of anger, frustration, and confusion. Sometimes a fight is necessary to create greater emotional distance or to break down walls of silence. Dialogue of feelings is the purpose. The goal is for both persons to *win*. It is not "I win, you lose." Nor is it, "You win, I lose." It is, "I win, you win." Enlightened self-interest is a valuable asset. If I hit too hard, it will hurt me in the long run. If I do not receive some of the blows solidly, she will not have got through to me.

Both of us win when we have really heard each other's gripes, reestablished our relationship, redefined lines of responsibility, or renegotiated the delicate balance of power. Do you remember when we were kids, how we would teeter-totter in the park? You could jump off when your partner was up in the air and let him crash. Or you could "fight" with each other, bumping the ground, tossing each other in the air a bit. But when the excitement was over and it was time to quit, it was best to get off together—both winners.

There are some valuable ways to conclude quarrels happily. *One way is to think of alternative courses of action.* Usually an argument comes from some sort of impasse. Nothing breaks it up like a fair proposal. Options give some fresh air to the situation. Instead of arguing over whether they should spend Christmas eve at his parents or at hers, a couple might decide to stay home with their children—then go visit the grandparents later on during the holidays. In our therapy groups, people are helpful in providing alternatives to couples who are stalemated in their positions.

One salesman, Bill Q., traveled most of the time. His wife Rachel was lonely and frightened when he was gone. For years the pattern argument had gone like this: "Please give up selling, Bill, so you can be home with me and the kids. They're growing up and they don't even know you." Bill's response always was, "Selling is my life. It's the only thing I know." In the therapy group, however, all sorts of alternatives were explored: a) find a job selling that would not take Bill out of town; b) have Rachel go with Bill part of the time; c) Rachel could get a job so that she wouldn't be so lonely. None of these suggestions seemed to work, but it did break the mind set. One night Bill and Rachel announced that they had spent an entire evening looking at his territory on the map. By changing the pattern of travel, Bill could be home every Wednesday night. Also, there were semiannual sales meetings where wives were

welcome, but, because of residual anger, Rachel had
never gone. But, and this was the clincher, weekends
had always been wasted. Bill spent Saturday and Sunday working on his reports. Rachel was angry. Now he
was going to do more paper work in the motels, and
save his weekends for the family. When they said all
this, you could see that both of them had suddenly
found new light at the end of a long black tunnel.

A lot of fights can be avoided. Early in our courtship, I was late for dates; it was a habit I picked up in
adolescence and it took me a long time to break it. I
was always amazed that Julia never said anything critical. (That very fact probably helped me break the
habit.) It was only after we were married that she admitted that she had been upset sometimes, but she had
asked herself, "Is this important enough for us to have
an argument over?" And she had decided no.

We need to be especially careful if there are exten-
uating circumstances. Is he unusually tired? Is she in a
menstrual period? Are there hidden issues? Now is the
time to use that good old "third ear" again. Last night
I was working on a difficult paper—difficult for me, at
least. I was angry, frustrated, upset. Suddenly I thought,
"What if someone should start a fight with me right
now? I would blow my stack I'm so nervous." Just
then Julia walked in the room. I decided to tell her.
She listened to me, smiled warmly, and walked back
out of the room. Smart girl, I thought. Nothing she
could have said at that moment would have been very
helpful. Besides, she took me seriously and left me
alone. No use having a fight over nothing.

I figure that Julia and I waste about five to ten dollars a month in bad decisions. We buy a pair of shoes
the day before a sale starts. We get a parking ticket, or
buy something in one store only to find it cheaper across
the street. We used to blame each other, in fact spend
time arguing about some incident. Now, most of the
time, a comment or two is enough. There is no use to

make a federal case out of it. Besides, tomorrow I'll be the guilty one.

Family Fights and the Christian Faith

What resources does a Christian marriage have that other marriages lack? In the first place, that residual anger against God, the world, or life itself is often melted in immediate experience of God's love. Married couples who wear emotional chips on their shoulders are in trouble from the start. Many a man or woman has experienced the acceptance of God in Jesus Christ, known that he is loved by a holy love, and been freed from a blind hostility that debilitates and destroys. The touch of the Spirit of Christ has quieted many an angry heart. Energy is not destroyed. The Spirit gives a new disciplined power which stimulates creativity.

The work of a Christian is helpful too. Karl Menninger has argued persuasively that the most powerful way to use up or drain hostility is to work. A couple who are so in love with Christ that they are working to witness and serve mankind have great amounts of their energy absorbed in self-forgetful service. Great tasks—great in the eyes of God—can make great marriages.

But in the tough times, we can hang on for Jesus' sake. Only the deeply committed believers will understand these words. The world and its philosophies will laugh or shake their heads. But those who know the mystery of his sacrifice and the claims which are laid upon us, find a hidden strength to survive. What does the fighter do when he is in trouble in the ring? Punch drunk, wobbly kneed, ready to go down, he gets into a clinch. He hangs on. In the dark nights of the soul —not with condescension or airs of superiority, not with a martyr complex, but with tenacious living and loving—the follower of Christ hangs on. Even in moments when, because of his own blindness, he sees nothing lovable in his mate, he nevertheless loves for Jesus' sake. Paul had something like that in mind when he wrote: "We are handicapped on all sides, but we are never frustrated; we are puzzled, but never in despair. We are persecuted, but never have to stand it alone: we may be knocked down, but we are never knocked out!" (II Cor. 4:8-9 Phillips).

7

The Bible and Woman's Lib

In Peter's First Letter to the churches, he wrote:

You married women should adapt yourselves to your husbands, so that even if they do not obey the Word of God they may be won to God without any word being spoken, simply by seeing the pure and reverent behavior of you, their wives. Your beauty should not be dependent on an elaborate coiffure, or on the wearing of jewelry or fine clothes, but on the inner personality—the unfading loveliness of a calm and gentle spirit, a thing very precious in the eyes of God. This was the secret of the beauty of the holy women of ancient times who trusted in God and were submissive to their husbands. Sarah, you will remember, obeyed Abraham and called him her lord. And you have become, as it were, her true descendants today as long as you too live good lives and do not give way to hysterical fears.

Similarly, you husbands should try to understand the wives you live with, honouring them as physically weaker yet equally heirs with you of the grace of eternal life. If you don't do this, you will find it impossible to pray properly. (I Pet. 3:1-7 Phillips)

Do you remember how funny it was in *Mary Poppins*, when Mrs. Banks pranced across the screen singing "Sister Suffragette"?

> Cast off the shackles of yesterday,
> Shoulder to shoulder into the fray.
> No more meek and mild subservients we,

We're fighting for our rights militantly.
Our daughters' daughters will adore us,
And they'll sing in grateful chorus,
"Well done, Sister Suffragette!"*

It was not quite so funny, however, on the fiftieth anniversary of the Proclamation of Woman's Suffrage, when twenty thousand women marched down Fifth Avenue. In Denver, women carried signs that read: "DON'T IRON WHILE THE STRIKE IS HOT!" Airline hostesses carried placards that said, "Storks fly, why can't mothers?" Some women invaded McCorley's ale house in New York, which has been an all-male bastion for 116 years. One woman had a stein of beer poured over her head. In Congress, a bill that had been introduced every year since 1923 was finally passed. It stated that "equality of rights under the law shall not be denied or abridged on account of sex."

The issue continues to bubble—even boil. I really think that there is woman's lib behind every bra—and even where there are no bras. Julia and I have had a lot of fun talking about the whole affair. We have sometimes become downright philosophical. Not long ago we went to a marriage enrichment-spiritual life camp. On the way home, we talked about the Bible and woman's lib. We decided to talk about it in front of the church. It was a dialogue sermon, and it went something like this:

Dick: Julie, women are trying to get into West Point and Annapolis. They're racing motorcycles and horses. They're waving bras and girdles in Chicago. What do you think about all this?

Julia: Some of it is ludicrous, of course. But some issues are very important. Take job opportunities and pay scales for example. A lot of jobs aren't open to women—just because they are women. And right in

* © 1963 Wonderland Music Company, Inc. Used by permission.

our hometown, women schoolteachers get less salary than men teachers—people with the same education and experience. It's a disgrace. Most of them are bread-winners too. I know widows, raising three and four children, who receive less money than the man teaching right across the hall.

Dick: I agree that wages ought to be equal for the same job. But surely the gals don't want all kinds of grubby, man-type jobs—like being grease monkeys and bulldozer operators?

Julia: Watch your words now. Don't you think it's a little grubby, cleaning out the oven at home—or scrubbing the kitchen floor or washing out messy diapers? Or is that "woman's work"? Besides, don't forget that your own aunt was a professional light plane pilot. She got plenty of grease on her hands disassembling Piper Cub engines. And look at the farm women on tractors—driving wheat trucks—helping their husbands. Maybe there are jobs we can't do or don't want, but *we* ought to be the ones to decide. We ought to have an equal chance at them. That reminds me, educational opportunities and professional opportunities are not equal either.

Dick: I was afraid you would get to that. My own alma mater, Yale University, finally opened the doors of its college to women, after a mere 250-year hesitancy. (Of course, they're still on a restricted percentage basis.) I'm sure that medical, dental, and law schools still make it rough on girls. We are definitely prejudiced against women pastors in the church. But don't you really think the woman makes the greatest contribution with her family in her own home?

Julia: You mean, "the woman's place is in the home?" I think that slogan is as outdated as a washboard. If you mean that a good wife needs to understand and encourage her husband, or that a good mother needs to provide for her children's emotional and physical and spiritual needs, then I would agree with you. But if you mean there is something sacred about sitting at home twiddling your thumbs, or washing the woodwork again, then that's ridiculous. Before our children were born, I would have gone crazy in that two-room garage apartment while you studied and worked all day and half the night. Besides what would we have had to eat, if I hadn't been teaching? I'd call that being supportive of my husband.

Dick: All right, but what about all the mothers who work? I read where 50 percent of all mothers in America are working outside the home. Surely some of the breakdown in family life is caused by that.

Julia: That's probably true. Oh, I could argue that some women are better wives and mothers because they get out of the house a few hours every day. Many women who work have their children in school or nearly grown. Mechanical aids, like washing machines and dishwashers and freezers, make housework a lot lighter. I could even argue that working women stimulate our economy, enrich our social fabric, and put vitality in our political scene. Yet in my heart, I know that many homes are being deprived of a wife's warmth and a mother's kindness and patience because she's either gone or all tired out.

Dick: I'm always glad to have you home. I hate to come home to an empty house. I know that the first thing the kids do when they hit the front door is to yell, "Mom!" Do you remember reading that book, *Bed & Board,* by Robert F. Capon? He claims that "Mother is a *place.*"[1] That's true around our house. Whenever you're gone for a day or two substitute teaching, things seem to fall apart and everybody gets edgy. Why do you think most wives work anyway?

Julia: Well, some of them have to. In addition to widows and divorcées, there are a lot of women whose husbands are ill, disabled, unemployed, or whose jobs just don't pay enough to feed the family and buy anything else. A lot of wives work in order to have more than the necessities—they want nice things. As a teacher friend of mine put it, "My husband brings home the bacon, and I bring home the gravy." Usually that is a pretty bad reason. These women, by the time they buy a second car, get some new working clothes, have their hair fixed every week, and pay the baby-sitter, spend about as much as they make. Besides that, they never have much time to enjoy what extra money they do have. You see them at the laundromat or shopping center weekends and evenings, rather than at home entertaining friends or at the lake using the speed boat they've just bought. They're too busy working or trying to catch up at home. However, Dick, I think that there is a deeper reason than any of these.

Dick: All right, I'm intrigued. What is it?

Julia: Our society is so materialistic. Money seems to be the answer to everything. So a woman, in a culture where the dollar is god, doesn't feel a sense of worth unless she is paid cash for her work. You start to feel that if you want to make a contribution to the family, you bring home a second paycheck. I feel that way myself when I bring home my substitute teacher's check. The kids were proud that Mom was making a monetary contribution to the family.

Dick: Wow! That means we don't express much appreciation for the value of your services in the home. Actually, from a purely financial viewpoint, you make a lot of money for us at home. If I had to hire the house cleaned or the clothes washed or the shirts ironed or baby-sitters, it would cost a bundle. When you mend a pair of pants or make one of the girls a dress, that's money in the bank. One of your famous casserole dishes is cheaper than a TV dinner—plus, there's no comparing the taste.

Julia: But nobody ever says that. Everything seems second-rate.

Dick: I'm going to start saying it.

Julia: Thanks. But it's more pervasive than that. We

wives have lost our self-confidence. Homemade is second-best. You know that little slogan from Pillsbury? "Nothin' says lovin' like somethin' from the oven." It would be OK if they would stop there, but then they tack on, "and Pillsbury says it best." The trouble is, they do. Anybody can make a box cake, and it really is better than most attempts from scratch. Canning peaches isn't really very profitable by the time you buy all the fruit and sugar and jars. Even most children's clothes are cheaper to buy than they are to make if you watch the sales. I'm taking a sewing course right now. Our main aim is to make things look "bought." The last thing we want is for a garment to look homemade. We've lost our sense of worth in the home. You can't imagine my thrill when Paul gave the grace at dinner and added to his prayer: "And bless the hands that prepared it." That made me feel good all over.

Dick: We husbands have a lot to learn about appreciation. I'm going to start reminding you of the money you've saved or made by your wifely efforts. But more than that, there are a lot of values that don't have a price tag. When you fix the kids a peanut butter and jelly sandwich after school, or when you have time to help the kids with their lessons, or when you're playing the piano when I come home—well, you can't put a dollar and cents price on that.

There is a familiar verse that shows how cloddish we husbands are with our inadequate expressions of appreciation.

> They were single and went walking,
> And her heart did skip a beat;
> As she stumbled on the sidewalk,
> He murmured, "Careful, Sweet."
>
> Now the wedding bells have rung,
> And when they walk the self-same street,
> When she stumbles on the sidewalk,
> He just yells, "Pick up your feet."

Julia: Another reason I'm almost ready to join Woman's Lib is their valid protest of the use of sex in advertising. Why does it take a girl in a bathing suit to sell crankcase oil? Shouldn't there be more to womanhood than just an object to be looked at? Besides, when you're thirty-five, it's hard to compete.

Dick: Now you're beginning to sound like St. Peter. He wrote that women ought not to be overly concerned with their outward appearance. He recommended concern for your spiritual qualities, for your personality and character."

Julia: Some churches have missed the point on that. They've gotten all excited about lipstick or earrings. They made a law out of it. A woman ought to look nice. But the Scripture is trying to make a valid point of emphasis. We ought not to be consumed with worry about the way we look. I can't go along with those who don't even comb their hair. We're not all Elizabeth Taylors, and I usually need all the help I can get. But I hope I'm a lot more of a person than mere appearances.

Dick: Julia, now let's really get to the heart of the matter. They burned Bibles in Berkeley because they said it was all written by men. Somewhere in this Woman's Lib movement there's a struggle concerning the husband and wife relationship. Sara is honored because she called Abraham her Lord. I haven't heard you calling me lord lately. In Peter's First Letter, he said that wives should be submissive to their husbands. Paul used that word "submissive" too. How does a tall, red-headed Texas spitfire get along with submissive?

Julia: No word in all Scripture has bothered me more. I know that Jesus Christ has done much for women. In ancient times and in other cultures, she is often a slave, a chattel mortgage, or at best, a second-class citizen. The New Testament is really the foundation for the emancipation of women. The faith of Mary, the resurrection witness of Mary Magdalene, the faithfulness of Lydia are part of our heritage. Besides, Paul said that in Christ there is neither male nor female. And in this same passage from First Peter, where the word "submissive is used, it says that wives are to be honored because they are equally heirs with men of the grace of eternal life.

The first help that I ever received was from a Bible scholar who said that the word really means "to throw a foundation under." Now, *that* really made sense. The word "submissive always sounded like "doormat," and I'm too independent to be a doormat for anyone. But "throw a foundation under" is exciting to a woman. The wife's role is a supporting role. It's a very important—even indispensable—role. I don't want to be the chief in our family. I don't want my husband to trail after me. I want my husband to be the head of our home. I'm a strong person, but I married a stronger husband.

Dick: Boy, I'm glad to get that in the record.

Julia: Of course, the Scriptures say some things about husbands, too.

Dick: I was afraid of that.

Julia: Paul expects the husband to assume leadership. Like Christ, he is to lay down his life for his wife. If he does that, it makes being supportive a lot easier. And Peter said you should try to understand us. I know that we women act like we always want our own way. But the truth is that, for the most part, we want the man to win. Oh, I don't mean that we want him to be brutish or authoritative or demanding. We don't want him to beat us up. We never tell him, of course—in fact it's one of those secret little things that men have to figure out on their own. We struggle for power, but inwardly we want them to take hold of the reins of leadership. We want to be secure in our homes, and we want our husbands to provide that security.

Dick: One of the things I've noticed about some of the woman's lib leaders is that they are often very hostile, angry people. This Kate Millett whom you were telling me about. . . .

Julia: Yes, her father had beat her as a child. Then he abandoned the family. Her mother had to go out and find work to support them. When I read the story of her life, I could easily understand why she had so much hatred toward men and why she felt that womans lib was her whole life.

Dick: I've been reading several of Dr. Karl Menninger's books. He says that the main reason for this kind of hostility is that men have failed to provide the kind of security, sexual satisfaction, and love which every woman wants and needs. Menninger gets his ideas from the human body itself, but his theory is that the woman is receptive, open, and capable of productive response. The man has responsibilities for providing the kind of warmth and security in which she is able to respond.

Julia: Exactly what Paul meant in Ephesians!

You wives must learn to adapt yourselves to your husbands, for the husband is the "head" of the wife in the same way that Christ is head of the Church. . . . The willing subjection of the Church to Christ should be reproduced in the submission [support] of wives to their husbands. But, remember, this means that the husband must give his wife the same sort of love that Christ gave to the Church, when he sacrificed Himself for her. . . . Men ought to give their wives the love they naturally have for their own bodies. The love a man gives his wife is the extending of his love for himself to enfold her. (Eph. 5:21-26 Phillips)

In the old German Lutheran style, on Sunday morning a family would go down the aisle of the church like this: the father would lead, then the oldest son, then the children, by order of age, then the wife. The father would stop by the pew, let all the children go in, beginning with the oldest, finally his wife and, last of all, himself. In that way his wife sat by the youngest child and next to him. That's leadership.

I want to wrap this up by telling a long, but beautiful story. It is Chaucer's *Wife of Bath's Tale*. Once upon a time, one of King Arthur's knights was "lustily riding home one day from hawking." He discovered a maiden in his path and raped her. The offense was so grave and the "outcry so keen" that Arthur was ready to take his life. The queen and her ladies begged that he be spared. So Arthur left the decision as to his fate up to the queen. She tells the knight that she will grant him his life if he can find the answer to the question "What is the thing that most of all women desire?" She gives him a year and a day to return to the castle.

After a hopeless year, he must return to face a death sentence. But on the final day, he encounters an ugly old woman (as ugly a witch as fancy could devise). Hearing of his troubles, she tells him she will give him the answer if he swears that he will do the one thing she will ask. Faced with the two alternatives (death or her request), he asks for the answer. She tells him the secret: "Most of all women desire to have the sovereignty and sit in rule and government above their husbands and to have their way in love."

The queen was fully satisfied with the answer, but now the witch demands that the knight marry her. The wedding night comes, and the knight lies in despair by her side, unable to overcome his revulsion at her ugliness. At last, the witch gives him two more alternatives: either accept her, ugly as she is, and she will be a true and humble wife to him all her life, or she will turn herself into a young and beautiful maiden, but will never be faithful to him. For a long time the knight ponders the two alternatives and decides to choose neither of them—he decides *not* to decide. At this moment the witch not only turns into a beautiful maiden, but into a faithful, obedient wife as well.

Dick, within every woman there is a desire to have sovereignty and to sit in rule above her husband. But that desire makes a witch of her, and it makes a man feel caught between impossible choices. When the knight finally made a decision of his own—took the leadership in choosing not to decide—he became free. And, the witch, who was really tied up in knots as well, became free, too.

Don't yield your leadership. Don't hand us the reins. We would consider this an abdication on your part. It would confuse us; it would alarm us; it would make us pull back. Quicker than anything else, it will fog the clear vision that made us love you in the first place. Oh, we will try to get you to give up your position as No. 1 in the house. That is the terrible contradiction in us. We will seem to be fighting you to the last ditch for final authority. But in the obscure recesses of our hearts we want you to lead.

8

For Everything
There Is a Season

For everything there is a season, and a time for every matter under heaven:
  A time to be born, and a time to die;
  a time to plant, and a time to pluck up what is
    planted; . . .
  a time to weep, and a time to laugh; . . .
  a time to embrace, and a time to refrain from
    embracing; . . .
  a time to keep silence, and a time to speak;
  a time to love, and a time to hate.

                    (Eccl. 3:1-2, 4, 5, 7)

A Time to Be Alone—Together

Here's a confession from a couple of fools. When
Julia and I were courting—we spent a lot of time
together. We studied in the library together. We went
to church together. We danced on Friday and Saturday nights together.

We used to park in the old athletic field near the
Southern Methodist University campus. Lots of
couples parked there. The campus police always
seemed to look the other way. We were alone. We
talked. We dreamed. We hugged and kissed. But the
world was right outside the windows, so we weren't
completely alone. We kept looking at our watches to
see when the girls' dorm would close. Wrapped in
each other's arms, we talked about having our own
bungalow. I took her to the dorm, kissed her good-

night, and turned and walked into the night. But I was thinking, "Someday, we'll really be alone— together."

But we were so dumb—after we got married. We married on a hot, muggy June night in Texarkana. By the time we had had a formal church wedding, greeted half the state of Arkansas and part of the state of Texas, eaten a dry ham sandwich, and driven to Magnolia, Arkansas, we were totally exhausted. We had five days to get to Connecticut. When we got there, Julia started summer school—already a week late. And I started moving freight and furniture.

But it was not the work. It was our attitudes. Before we knew it we were in a frenzy of activity. Mostly it took us in separate directions. We did very little together. Almost imperceptibly we each began to get up-tight about our individual responsibilities. Were we suddenly afraid of being together in some unhurried atmosphere? Or did we think we could show love by being overly conscientious?

During the next few years, I became preoccupied with seminary studies and church work. Julia became pregnant and was sick for months. Slowly we found it harder and harder to communicate. Once we had spent whole evenings just talking. Now that we were married, we were too busy or too tired. Where were the long walks in the park we had dreamed about? Or what happened to the evenings when the two of us could curl up in front of the fire, eat a bowl of popcorn, and be all by ourselves? I'll tell you what happened: we forgot. We forgot our dream. We forgot how important it was. We forgot how necessary it is to play and execute a happy time together—without people or thoughts crowding in.

I talked the other day to a fellow who spent his honeymoon in the Bahamas. I said, "Wow." He said that he and his bride were there for three months. I said, "Double wow." Then he admitted that her parents lived in the Bahamas, and they spent the entire three months living with them. I said, "Oh." He said, "Yeah! It was three months of hell."

Now maybe I am not talking to everybody. I'm sure that there are couples sitting in the grass drinking wine and eating cheese who need to be told to get up and go to work. Maybe there are couples who are together so much in work and in play that they are satiated with each other. Maybe so. But I know of scores of marriages where they desperately need a date once a week. They need to have some fun togther.

The turning point of our marriage happened in the fifth year. We agreed to leave our two babies at home, hire a baby-sitter, and go to a spiritual life retreat. Another pastor was responsible for the services at the church; we had no responsibilities at the camp. We studied together and prayed together and walked together and slept together. We experienced God together. And we learned that "for everything there is a season." Since that time, we have tried to have an evening once a week plus a little time each day that is *ours*.   . .

Charlie Shedd, that skillful author of letters to his children, writes in *Letters to Karen*: "In one vital marriage I know, the husband and wife have what they call their 'little deal.' They say, 'It turned out to be one of the biggest deals we ever made!' They promised each other that they would take a few minutes at bed-time to share this question, "What was the happiest moment of your life today?"

Shedd continues, "Other couples have agreed to at least one meal out together each week. They allow for a baby-sitter in their budget and set aside funds for dinner at one of their favorite eating places. Social events with others do not count. These are their moments alone to 'focus their souls.' "[1] Every married couple needs to learn this, and the sooner the better.

When it comes to dangerous fish, most people are

afraid of the sharks. They fear that one of these denizens of the deep will swoop in and devour them. But there is another fish that is much more dangerous. It is the piranha. It is tiny, but it nibbles and nibbles, and soon nothing is left but the skeleton.

It is true that a single decision, a gross betrayal, a sellout can destroy a marriage. But more frequent and more dangerous is the day-by-day loss of dialogue. Dullness nibbles at love; routine eats away at vital relationships. Soon the dream is gone. Some of the saddest marriages ever to drift into a counselor's office are couples who have been married twenty years. They do not know when it started, but somewhere, years ago, they began to drift apart. They forgot, somewhere along the line, that there is a time to be together—alone. Good marriages don't just happen. They require attention.

A Time to be Apart—Alone

Inevitably, those thinking about marriage emphasize togetherness. But the parallel truth is important too. There is a time to be apart. Although each person is different, everybody needs some time to be alone. "There is a time to embrace, and a time to refrain from embracing." Kahlil Gibran put it beautifully:

> But let there be spaces in your togetherness,
> And let the winds of the heavens dance between you.
> Love one another, but make not a bond of love:
> Let it rather be a moving sea between the shores
>   of your souls.[2]

Paul may have known more about marriage than people give him credit for. When he said that couples should refrain from sex during times of agreed-upon prayer, he put his finger on something. He was not just talking about prayer and sex; he was talking about being apart for a while.

I remember some years ago sailing across the Atlantic on the *Queen Elizabeth* (a pity she is no more). I had been married only a couple of years and I thought the six-weeks' absence would be unbearable. One day, I decided to get a haircut aboard ship. The barber started telling me about his wife and children. Suddenly I felt very sorry for him, crossing the ocean all the time, being apart from his family. "It must be rough," I said, "being gone all the time."

"Oh no," he grinned, "I'm gone for two weeks and home for a week. It's like a honeymoon every time I go home."

We have to step back from each other from time to time. We need what the psychologists call distance. Nothing gives me a better perspective on my marriage than to be apart for a day or two—sometimes even longer. When I'm sleeping on a bedroll in some church basement or eating at a cafe while attending a series of meetings, I can feel an appreciation of home welling up within me. That is why wives shouldn't complain when their husbands go on fishing trips. If the men do not get nagging when they leave or criticism when they come home, they will be better husbands for having made the trip. At least *most* of the time, home cooking is better than campfire food. And the bed at home *ought* to be softer than sleeping on the ground.

Wives too need to get away for a while, even if it is only for a few hours. Anne Morrow Lindbergh, busy mother of five and the wife of the famous pilot, Charles Lindbergh, takes a few days from time to time to live alone on a small island. In solitude, she is spiritually restored. In her meditation, *Gift from the Sea,* she writes:

I want . . . to be at peace with myself. I want a single-ness of eye, a purity of intention, a central core to my life that will enable me to carry out my obligations as well as I can. . . .

I must find a balance somewhere . . . between solitude and communion, between retreat and return.

If one is out of touch with oneself, then one cannot touch others . . . Only when one is connected to one's own core is one connected to others. . . . For me, the core, the inner spring, can best be refound through solitude.[3]

Distance requires a time apart. It may be for a few minutes, a few hours, or a few days. It may be for pleasure, for work, or for prayer. It is too bad if we always wait for a fight before we are aware that we are getting on each other's nerves. We shouldn't need an argument before we recognize that a little distance is required. We ought to be smart enough to build a little of it into the normal pattern of our lives.

I recently read a clever article in *Marriage Magazine* entitled "Down with Dialog."[4] It turned out that it really wasn't an attack on depth dialogue—that kind of open, caring communication we have been discussing. Rather, it fired a broadside at too much conversation, too much togetherness—and it made a good point. Robert Louis Stevenson once remarked that marriage is one long conversation. I do not know what *his* wife was like, but for me, there had better be some long pauses.

Prayer can be a significant way of stepping aside and gaining perspective. Julia and I sometimes kneel beside our bed and pray together. We hold hands in church during the prayers. But most of the time we pray alone. There are issues deeper than marriage. There is loneliness that no human being can satisfy. Sometimes we have to talk to the Lord.

We asked each person in our marriage therapy groups to set aside a time each day for prayer. It is a specified discipline which is a part of the Yokefellow Prayer Therapy program. It calls for a half-hour period each day for private meditation and prayer. We found that the prayer time was a vital key in our effort to restructure relationships.

A wise couple builds into their family life times when each person can have some quiet, private thoughts. It is a stronger home when everyone has personal spiritual resources, which, though garnered in solitude, find expression in family living.

A Time to Weep and a Time to Laugh

Nobody ever said that married life was easy. Abraham had his troubles; so did King David. Jesus evidently chose the single life so that he could devote full intensity to his brief ministry, unencumbered by the responsibilities of wife and family.

It has always taken time and effort—and tears—to raise a family. Sometimes I walk around in one of our old Kansas cemeteries—ones that go back into the 1860s and '70s and '80s. The stones are often limestone. Many have crumbled and are nearly illegible. You find a lot of children's graves. Over here are three sisters, age one, two, and four, carried off by smallpox in 1882. Over there are twins, buried together after an epidemic. A lot of young women who died in childbirth are buried in those old sections under the cedar trees.

It has always been tough. Dads have always gotten gray hair looking after a wife and kids. Mothers have always become a little bent from taking care of a husband and family. There have been unemployment lines before and loose sex and too much drinking and loneliness. The couples who built sod houses on these Kansas prairies and tried to raise families in spite of grasshoppers and dust and disease never argued that it was easy.

But our times have their struggles too. In some ways, maybe it is harder to make it today. Roles are not so clear. Values are confused. Pressures are severe. Few marriage books say it, but you've got to "hang-tough" to make a go of it. Take sex, for instance. With all the sensuousness of our culture, with all the puritan hang-ups of our up-bringing, it is no wonder we suffer. Many a man walks out of his bedroom at night, frustrated and angry. Many a woman weeps in the midnight hours, misunderstood and lonely. That is pain. Some marriages struggle with that for years.

Or take mixed backgrounds. I've been trying to learn to like okra and turnip greens for twenty years, but they will never replace mashed potatoes and gravy. There are hundreds of thousands of racially mixed marriages—and there are going to be more. That is a rocky road to travel. There are more Catholic-Protestant marriages than ever before; some call them ecumenical marriages now. Although the churches are cooperating more (for which I thank God), couples still carry a lot of emotional freight into that kind of marriage. When a beer-drinking Polish Catholic farm boy marries a teetotaling Southern Baptist city girl, there is going to be stress.

Raising kids is not easy. With drive-in movies and drugs, even the best of families can lose touch. A number of years ago a Methodist college claimed that it was built "fourteen miles from the nearest form of temptation." It is difficult to find a place like that anymore. Our oldest son is at the dating age. Now Julia and I read late at night, yawning, and hoping to hear the car pull in the driveway. I notice that there is more gray in her hair now.

We have stressed that being vulnerable is a key to dialogue. When you are open—and you must be to love—sometimes you get hurt. Nobody knows *you* as well as your mate. When he (or she) sticks the knife in your ribs and turns it, it cuts. It hurts worse than from anybody else.

One reason I believe in the Christ of the Cross is because there is a cross at the very center of life. Those who try to avoid it, live on life's periphery.

God's love includes suffering. All love contains pain. "In love's labors, only the wounded can serve."

Our goal is to grow, to survive, to win. Dr. Harry Fosdick once said, "Joy is not mostly pleasure, it is mostly victory." To go through the valleys and come up on the hillside again is the hope of every marriage. Let's take some of the moonlight and roses out of our marriage myths. We'd soon get tired of it if it were real, anyway. Robert Speaight, English journalist and lecturer, once said, "Too many people want liberty without discipline, life without death, adventure without risk!"

Usually we think of joy and sorrow as antithetical. If we thought of joy and sorrow as people, we would figure that they lived on opposite sides of town. We would think of ourselves as living neighbors to one or to the other. But the truth is that we learn through agony. We are healed through pain. Sorrow is the wood out of which our house of joy is built. Just as the Negro spirituals were born in the cotton rows of slavery, so some great marriages have risen out of trials and tribulations. We ought to anticipate pain in our marriage and not be surprised by it. It takes guts to stay married. . . . There will be many crises between the wedding day and the golden anniversary, and the people who make it are heroes.[5]

I remember when our babies were born. I can still hear my wife's cries. I remember our two miscarriages, the feeling of loss, and the tears. I remember Julia's strong grip in the pains of labor. But I remember too the look on her face as she cradled a child in her arms. I remember kissing her and receiving a warm sweet kiss that smelled of ether. When I look into the faces of our children today, I haven't forgotten, nor has she, but we give thanks to God. It's worth it.

Gibran's poetry catches something of the mysterious intimacy between hurt and happiness. Think about your own marriage and see if it isn't true.

Then a woman said, Speak to us of Joy and Sorrow.
And he answered:
Your joy is your sorrow unmasked.
And the selfsame well from which your laughter rises
was oftentimes filled with your tears.
And how else can it be?
The deeper that sorrow carves into your being, the more
joy you can contain.
Is not the cup that holds your wine the very cup that
was burned in the potter's oven?
And is not the lute that soothes your spirit, the very
wood that was hollowed with knives?
When you are joyous, look deep into your heart and
you shall find it is only that which has given you
sorrow that is giving you joy.
When you are sorrowful look again in your heart, and
you shall see that in truth you are weeping for that
which has been your delight.
Some of you say, "Joy is greater than sorrow," and
others say, "Nay, sorrow is the greater."
But I say unto you, they are inseparable.
Together they come, and when one sits alone with you
at your board, remember that the other is asleep
upon your bed.[6]

In marriage, as in life, joy is not mostly pleasure, it is
mostly victory. There really is a time to weep and a
time to laugh.

9

Love Story Reborn

Can things get better? Can good marriages improve? Is it possible for stagnant relationships to bubble into fresh enthusiasm? What about marriages that are about to go on the rocks? Can they have a new lease on life? The answer is a resounding YES. But it requires a bit of doing.

We first have to get our standards straight. Marriage is a matter of top priority. If we succeed in marriage, we succeed in life, no matter how many failures we have in other areas. If we fail in marriage, all the successes in the world will not compensate for the disappointment. The welfare of our children is uppermost in our minds. Normally, we are successful in raising our kids if we do a good job expressing love within our marriages. We usually foul up with our kids if we mess up the husband-wife relationship. One man has this motto on his desk to help him remember:

> The most important thing a father
> can do for his children is
> to love their mother.

The marriage relationship is central, integral, bedrock. The Bible even claims that a woman can gain salvation through the faith of her husband. A man can be saved through the obedience of his wife. Nothing in this world deserves our higher attention. As one wedding ceremony declares: "No other human ties are more tender, no other vows more sacred."[1]

Sick Marriages

Of course, some marriages are in *bad trouble*. Dialogue is so shattered, the trust level is so low, that decisive action is demanded. For these couples—and their number is legion—let me offer some concrete suggestions:

a) Do not wait too long. Sick marriages are like sick people. It is easier to cure them early. By the time people get in a divorce court or somebody has a nervous breakdown, things have gotten eleventh hourish. That is when you start praying for miracles. Miracles can happen, but the odds are low.

b) Keep the relatives and friends out of it. What a sick marriage needs is a touch of objectivity. I have yet to observe a troubled marriage which was helped by solicitous parents or compassionate friends. There is too much involvement, too much emotion already. Somebody needs to enter the scene who is outside the dynamics (sorry, mothers). Even counselors and pastors refer a couple they know extremely well to somebody else.

c) Do your best to go together. That is a hard request to make of two people who are not cooperating, but it is vital. Most young men are hesitant to receive help. They are too damn proud. They think, "If only "she'd get off my back," or If only she'd warm up in bed," everything would be all right. Encouragement from an older man may help. Depressed people are difficult to get into a counseling situation. They are so blue, emotionally drained, that they cannot function effectively. That makes it hard for them to make a decision. One mate may need to take a very strong leadership role. Professional people are the worst. A doctor, a lawyer, a minister, who is familiar with all the procedures—or thinks he is—will think of a million excuses. He is afraid that people will find out he is not perfect. Those who help others are sometimes unable to receive help themselves. One young attorney, whose wife was pleading for help, let his marriage go completely on the rocks rather than walk inside another professional's door.

Avoid negative approaches. Threats are not helpful. A statement like, "If you don't go with me to see my minister, I'm going to leave you," may cause you to pack your suitcase. Accusations and demands are futile. "Sister, *you* need help. Our home life is going to be miserable until you get straightened out. You need to go to a head shrinker." A sounder approach (which actually is a form of dialogue, and, unfortunately, requires more "cool" than most distressed people have) goes like this. "Baby, we're in a hell of a mess. Things are not going right for us. We need somebody to give us a hand. I'm willing to go to anybody you are—family counselor, priest or minister, chaplain, or psychologist. Let's do something before it's too late."

d) Go to a recognized, reputable, trained person. It is intelligent to make a few inquiries. Your family physician may have a recommendation; so might your pastor. Many pastors, both Catholic and Protestant, are now receiving special training. Not all are qualified however, and not all of them feel adequately experienced in this type of ministry. Chaplains in general hospitals and psychiatric centers usually know the best resources available. Many cities now have family guidance centers. Find out how well staffed they are, how heavy their work load is. In marriage problems psychiatric care is not normally needed. Psychiatrists are trained to treat sick, dysfunctional people. If this treatment is needed, your professional counselor would probably make the referral.

There are some quacks around—defrocked ministers or priests who have hung up a shingle or fly-by-night

untrained "psychologists." They make their living prey-
ing on troubled people.

e) Go as you would go to a doctor. Go expecting a
diagnosis and a proposed method of treatment. Do not
go expecting advice—you can get that from the newspaper. Do not expect answers. Do not go expecting to
build a case against your mate, trying to prove you are
right. Your need is for someone to step in and alter the
dynamics of your relationship. Do not be surprised if
he suggests weekly interviews—maybe for a period of
months. (Crying on the counselor's shoulder for a few
minutes may be helpful, but it is not marriage therapy.)
Do not be surprised if a group sharing experience is
suggested. More and more pastors and counselors are
using marriage enrichment classes and marriage therapy
groups as a "medicine of choice."

It should cost you something—in money, time, and
effort. Counselors in private practice are expensive, but
no more expensive than a doctor. Community services
are usually based on your ability to pay. Most pastors
and churches do not charge a fee (though they probably should). However, if you give regular contribu-
tions to that church, regardless of your religious affilia-
tion, you help make that specialized ministry possible.
My thinking is this: if you had cancer, you would go to
a specialist, fly to Mayo clinic, take off three months of
work, do anything to save your life. Why should a
couple balk at an hour interview a week, or a once a
week therapy group, with some modest financial obli-
gation, in order to save their home?

f) Expect it to hurt and take time. There is pain in
change. It hurts to modify relationships. If you are
driving your car in a rut on a muddy road, there is
kind of a wrench when you pull out of it. Worn patterns of interaction take a certain amount of jolt to
change. That takes time too. No pastor, no counselor
has a magic wand that he can wave over a marriage of
twenty years and make it well. It took a long time to

get sick; it takes a while for it to get well. It requires hard work to restructure a relationship.

One last comment: after a good number of years of training and experience, after working in depth with scores of desperately troubled couples, I always have hope when both husband and wife earnestly seek help. Even if it is "five minutes before midnight," maritally speaking, even if they have committed adultery, threatened to shoot each other, attempted suicide, thrown everything at each other but the kitchen stove, or said words that would make a chief petty officer blush, there is hope as long as two people admit they are in trouble and are willing to ask for some responsible person to assist them.

To quote Reuel Howe again: "Dialogue can restore a dead relationship. Indeed, this is the miracle of dialogue: it can bring relationship into being, and it can bring into being once again a relationship that has died."[2]

Although countless thousands of couples need immediate help, the majority of marriages are rocking along pretty well. Yet many of us want to improve, start afresh, turn over a new leaf. What are the options? What must be done to make the love story perk up again?

Acceptance

Urban Steinmetz, marriage counselor and founder of the Family Enrichment League, gives a fascinating description of the trail toward mature love in his recorded talks on marriage. He lists five stages in the normal, everyday marriage: the dream world, disillusion, misery, awakening, and mature love.[3] It is good for couples to hear talks like these—some couples who are experiencing a letdown, think they are the only ones who have troubles. It is a relief to know that others have thorns on their rosebushes too. But Urb's big point is that marriages do not begin to mature until husbands and wives *quit trying to change each other*. He calls that "awakening." A healthy love starts emerging when man and wife learn to accept each other, *just the way they are*. After ten years of trying to get him to quit putting bread in his milk or drinking the soup from his bowl, the wife finally figures it's no use, and decides to accept him just the way he is. After innumerable requests for her to please be ready to go places on time— and after consistently waiting five or ten minutes while she finishes the last minute touch-ups, hubby finally learns to sit down and read the paper (sometimes he tells a lie about the time they're really supposed to be there). Does he forget to wear his overshoes when it rains? Well, his mother told him for twenty years; you have told him for twenty years. Maybe he is never going to learn. Does she still fail to put enough salt on the fried chicken? After you have told her a thousand times. That just may be the way it's going to stay. Some intelligent people decide that it is not worth bickering over any more.

My grandfather chewed tobacco. He chewed Sparkplug tobacco and spit into a Folgers coffee can. It was a mess, particularly when we were driving in the car and he tried to spit out the window. Grandmother tried to break him for forty years. Finally she got him to try to smoke cigarettes. He tried valiantly for several months, but it was no use. I will never forget, shortly before their golden wedding anniversary, when Grandmother said, "Well, I guess he can't change. I'm just going to have to live with it."

We do not change other people. When we finally quit trying, everybody relaxes and is a lot happier. The young woman who marries, figuring that she will change her husband into the man she always wanted, is in for a sad disillusionment. But when she accepts him, thinks that he is a pretty nice guy in spite of his faults, then a mature love emerges.

We begin to accept other people as we learn to accept ourselves. A person who is so insecure that he cannot relax with himself finds it difficult to accept someone else. The Danish philosopher, Soren Kierkegaard, wrote, "Even what one might call the poorest personality is everything when he has chosen himself; for the great thing is not to be this or that, but to be oneself."[4]

Self-acceptance ultimately depends upon experiencing the acceptance of God. Those who continually strive to measure up to a quota of rules are anxiety-ridden. They usually try to make other people measure up too. They are miserable to live with. Unfortunately, we have a lot of people like this in our churches. They think they are religious people. They are like Paul before he was converted, like Wesley before he felt his sins forgiven. Women who feel they are not "good" enough, keep the kind of houses where you are afraid to sit down for fear of wrinkling a pillow. Fathers who cannot accept themselves come home and immediately give the children ten chores to do before they say "hello."

The Christian faith is a tribute to the unqualified acceptance of God. We call it grace. It is the profound trust that Almighty God loves us in spite of ourselves. Christ's sacrifice is a divine yes-vote for us. It brings us into the family of God. The tragedy for so many is that they cannot, to use Paul Tillich's phrase, "accept their acceptance." Many Christian people have not appropriated that acceptance and continue to lash themselves. They strike out at others in constant criticism and condemnation.

Strangely enough, once we experience acceptance, we *want* to change. As long as we are being pushed, we dig our heels into the ground. Many a man would rather die than quit doing something his wife has been bitching about. When she accepts him as he is, and he accepts her as she is, the irritations become less important. It is a lot happier around the house. And, who knows, somebody might actually decide to do something differently. The greatest motivation for change comes from within.

Here is an example out of a pastoral visit. I called on an elderly grandmother whose husband had died some months before. He had been a great churchman. She told an interesting story. When they were first married he would not go to church at all. He slept late on Sunday, got up but did not shave, read the papers, and drank coffee. As a young bride, she decided to dress quietly, put the coffeepot on, lay the paper on the kitchen table, go off to church by herself, come home, and prepare a nice Sunday dinner. She never said a word to her husband about church. When the children came along, she got them dressed, took them to church, came home, and fixed dinner for everybody. Then one Sunday morning it happened. When she got up he was already shaving. As she started dressing the kids, he put on his suit. Finally she said, "What are you doing?" His reply is classic husband. "Getting ready for church, of course." For the next forty years, the couple worshipped together each Sunday.

The sequel is just as magnificent. Her granddaughter came to her shortly after her marriage and—you guessed it—said her young husband would not go to church with her. Grandmother retold the story of her early marriage, emphasizing the fact that she ought to make everything comfortable and happy for him on Sunday morning—no criticism—but go regularly and faithfully herself. You can imagine the gleam in Grandma's eye when she told me the same results had taken place. Her granddaughter's husband was now a deacon in the church.

Forgiveness and Being Forgiven

There is a line near the end of Eric Segal's *Love Story,* which goes, "Love means not ever having to say you're sorry." That was the theme song of the movie, too. Do you think it's true? An interviewer asked the actor who spoke the line in the movie what *he* thought it meant. The young actor said he never understood what the meaning was. I suppose a relationship can exist in which a person, eyes on ground, says, "I'm sorry," all the time. That sort of stance is a milk-toast, perpetually penitent, doormat attitude. It is bad psychology, bad religion, bad love. If that is what the expression meant, it may have a point.

But I do not think a marriage can survive without somebody saying, "I'm sorry." Without it, our ship would have gone under a long time ago. There have been nights when I have crawled out of a cold bed, knelt down in prayer, and said things to the Lord like this: "Lord, she's impossible, help her if you can. For all the things she's done and said, I hope you'll forgive her. Give me patience. It's obvious I'm going to need a lot of it."

I looked up and noticed that Julia still had her face to the wall. It seemed as if my prayers were bouncing off the ceiling.

I tried another approach: "Dear God, what's the matter with us? We can't seem to talk, or understand each other. She's been hard as nails, and I've said some things I really didn't mean." I thought I heard her move a little bit in bed. There seemed to be a small crack in the ceiling. A little light seemed to be shining through.

"Oh God, I'm so insensitive, so selfish. I've said things I wouldn't say to a stranger. Forgive me, and help to make things right again. I've been such a fool." It seemed as if the Lord leaned close enough to hear. When I got back up into the bed, and whispered in her ear, "I'm sorry," the wall of ice melted, tears began to flow, and dialogue commenced with infant steps. Tennyson described such a making-up:

> And blessings on the falling out
> Which all the more endears,
> When we fall out with those we love,
> And kiss again with tears.

One of the most delightfully true stories I ever heard was from the father of two girls. One night he came home and discovered a major offense. He grabbed the girl he thought was the guilty party, gave her a licking and sent her to bed. Later on, after a little detective work, he discovered that the other daughter was totally responsible. He had made a serious error. Slowly he went into his seven-year-old child's room, sat down next to her sobbing frame, and told her what he had found out. Then he said words that most parents forget to say. He said he had made a bad mistake, and that he was truly sorry. He hoped that she would forgive him. That little girl got up, wiped the tears from her eyes, gave her daddy a big hug, and smiled. "Daddy, I forgive you," she said. "We all make mistakes." My friend claims he could almost see his daughter grow taller.

When the church is truly alive and refreshing people, it gives opportunity and encouragement for couples to say to each other and to God, "I'm sorry." Husbands and wives are people, and they need to drain the crankcases of their souls. I have seen couples who were estranged, guilty of grievances against each other and God, unacceptable to themselves, kneel together before the altar. I could remember words spoken in the counseling session—words that spit in the face of love, but I could see them reach out, hold hands, and surrender to the Lord who forgives. With mutual forgiveness I have seen them take the bread and the wine. It is a healing that the world cannot give.

Breaking the Patterns

Dr. Harris, in *I'm OK, You're OK,* draws heavily on the experimental work of Dr. Wilder Penfield of McGill University in Montreal, Canada.

Dr. Penfield, a brain surgeon, touched different cells of the brain with electrical impulses. Thus stimulated, those memory cells responded with information which had been "forgotten." Childhood experiences, trivial memories, mental pictures beyond recall, all were remembered. Dr. Penfield concluded that everything we have ever given our attention to is recorded on the high fidelity tape recorder we call a brain. But more significant, as people remembered, they had the same *feelings* that they experienced originally. That means, in our brains, that the *feelings* of the past are tied to the *memories* of the past. If a person remembered a fireside and laughter and steaming turkey on Christmas Eve, his remembered feelings were happy, warm, and affectionate.

Now, lest someone think that argues for determined behavior—as if we just daily play back the tape—Dr. Harris argues that our present thoughts and our ideas about the future have a part to play. That is, our thoughts and hopes affect our behavior and our feelings. A fireman or a doctor might recall pleasant memories of Christmas Eve, yet decide, because of his job, to go to work this Christmas Eve, even though it meant leaving his warm hearth and family.

Now this seeming excursion is right on target for marriages. We need to be aware that we carry into our marriages a lot of memories with their locked-in feelings. These feelings can be triggered, just as surely as if the brain cell were stimulated. With a word or an action, we can call to mind old memories and old feelings.

It is critically important that we learn how to avoid getting "hooked," or "hooking" each other, in old, bad feelings. Last night I ate in a restaurant. A couple in their fifties sat across from me. They seemed happy until they got their menus. She said, "Oh there's a special on fish. I'm going to have fish. Aren't you going to have fish?" Without warning, he slammed down his menu, and said, loud enough for half the dining room to hear, "Look, you get what you want, I'll get what I want, OK?" She had come on as a little "parent" and hooked his "little boy" feelings. I could not help but think about the sadness of it all. They had been married thirty years, and they still played the same little game. Oh, they got over it and acted civilized the rest of their evening out. But what a tragedy that she still pressed the sensitive button, and he still responded with anger.

In marriage, it is easier to stop pressing the button than it is to stop responding. But both are possible. Change can take place whenever people want to change. When we hurt enough or when we are bored with the status quo or when we discover that we can change, we will. Wouldn't it have been intelligent for this woman, somewhere along the line to have learned to say, "I believe I'll get the special, what are you going to get?" Or maybe she could have just simply ordered her own meal. It is harder for him, but he could learn not to get hooked, and say, "It's true that there's a special, but I'm hungry for roast beef and I believe I'll get that."

My appeal is for an awareness of the other person's sensitive areas. There aren't too many of them. Why not look at them like somebody's feet in a movie theater? Try not to step on them.

We need so much from one another. We need to sidestep the tender spots; we need to provide positive fortification. Julia and I bought one of the colorful new banners to hang in our bedroom. It reads:

EACH OF US IS THE ONLY PERSON
WHO CAN GIVE THE OTHER
WHAT EACH OF US WANTS TO HAVE

Judith Viorst looks into her own marriage, spots the places where she and her husband get hooked over and over. In a delightful poem, "Maybe We'll Make It," she suggests there is really the possibility, after all this time, of sidestepping a few of the touchy places.

> If I quit hoping he'll show up with flowers, and
> He quits hoping I'll squeeze him an orange, and
> I quit shaving my legs with his razor, and
> He quits wiping his feet with my face towel, and
> We avoid discussions like
> Is he really smarter than I am, or simply more glib,
> Maybe we'll make it.

> If I quit looking to prove that he's hostile, and
> He quits looking for dust on the tables, and
> I quit inviting Louise with the giggle, and
> He quits inviting Jerome with the complex, and
> We avoid discussions like
> Suppose I died, which one of our friends would he
>   marry,
> Maybe we'll make it. . . .

> If I quit clearing the plates while he's eating, and
> He quits clearing his throat while I'm speaking, and
> I quit implying I could have done better, and
> He quits implying he wishes I had, and
> We avoid discussions like
> Does his mother really love him, or is she simply one of
>   those over-possessive, devouring women who can't
>   let go,
> Maybe we'll make it.[5]

Entering Dialogical Fellowships

For those who want to light a fire in their marriage, let me offer one last suggestion: become a part of a group where people know how to share. All of us need development in the ability to communicate. Join with some others in a group that has this goal as one of its purposes.

All sorts of groups are springing up throughout the country. There are countless formats, but, if the group is alive, it contains the dialogical elements which we have been discussing. There are marriage enrichment groups. Bible study groups, and sharing fellowships. There are sophisticated experiences in human relations. There are listening groups and young married classes. There are ecumenical living-room dialogue groups. A few of these groups are dead; but most are alive. Their life depends on their openness, their honesty, their degree of trust and acceptance.

The marvelous fact is that there are thousands of such fellowships. Unbelievable numbers of couples are experiencing depth dialogue with others—often with four or five couples like themselves. Most of the groups use some input material—a study book, a set of records, the Bible, or a mutually agreed upon theme. They strive for a sharing of thoughts that is personal, experiential, open. It is not a gossip session. Nor is it an intellectual game where ideas are tossed around. People talk about important matters and own up to their feelings. Time is disciplined. Many groups included prayer as part of their dialogue.

Good materials are available. The Family Enrichment Bureau has tapes and cassettes for a series of meetings or for ongoing groups. Churches have prepared springboard materials. Human relations labs, Bell and Howell for example, have produced excellent marriage and communications materials.

Longer experiences are also being developed. Spiritual life retreats, marriage enrichment weekends, family camps are springing up. Most of these are undergirded by sound psychological principles and spiritual awareness. Julia and I enjoy leading one or two marriage enrichment weekends each year.

The important thing is not that people need to learn more *about* marriage. or *about* communications or *about* human relations. We need to grow in *actual ability to communicate*. Our hunger is to become increasingly dialogical with people and with God (the two really do seem to go together). I am just about fed up with experts who write psychological textbooks but who have a lousy family life. Julia and I are both tired of church meetings that claim to be on the theme of fellowship or prayer, but are stilted, highly structured, and monological. One more human relations lab where somebody gives a lecture on interpersonal dynamics is *not* what we need.

Group life is happening. You can be part of it. People are meeting together, usually in homes, and are finding companionship, as husbands and wives share together. It is no longer the men in one room talking about sports, and the women in another room gabbing about the children. It is couples intimately talking about love and fear and guilt and death and loneliness and faith. The Yokefellow Prayer Therapy Program uses psychological testing and prayer disciplines. It has had over forty thousand groups. But open dialogical fellowships can start anywhere—wherever two or three couples want to begin.

The secret is a husband and a wife who care enough to want to grow. It is a tough world in which to build a vital marriage. We need the help of other people. We need the help of God. We need to care so much about deepening our love, that we will be attentive to each aspect of our intimate conversation together.

An open, caring, dialogical person gave us this anonymous verse:

Precaution

They say a wife and husband, bit by bit
Can rear between their lives a mighty wall.
So thick they cannot speak with ease through it,
Nor can they see across, it stands so tall.
Its nearness frightens them, but each alone
Is powerless to tear its bulk away;
And each, heartbroken, wishes he had known
For such a wall the magic word to say.

So let us build with master art, my dear,
A bridge of faith between your life and mine—
A bridge of tenderness and very near—
A bridge of understanding, strong and fine:
Till we have built so many lovely ties,
There never will be room for walls to rise.

From where Julia and I stand—looking back and looking forward—it's well worth the struggle.

Discussion Questions

Chapter I   Moonlight and Roses

1. How is *your* marriage different from that of your grandparents?
2. Did you go through a period of disillusionment when your romantic illusions collapsed? Do you have periodic relapses?

Chapter II   Dialogue Is the Key

1. From the Bible, read John 3:1-15. Did true dialogue take place?
2. Does dialogue occur in your marriage? When, usually?

Chapter III   The Third Ear

1. Do you know what the author means by "being fully present"? Are you successful at this?
2. How good a detective are you in your marriage? How good a detective is your mate in finding out what you are trying to say?
3. Do you and your wife/husband ever act as psychiatrists for one another?

Chapter IV   Eyes and Sighs

1. From the Bible, read Mark 14:22-25. What is being communicated symbolically?
2. Do you have any "vacuum cleaner" language? What are some of your symbols that tell of love? Of anger?

Chapter V   Sex Is God's Idea

1. Do you agree with the author's interpretation of Scripture, that sex is God's idea?
2. Were you taught that sex is beautiful? Ugly? Fun? Sacred?
3. Do you think that "swingers" have more fun in the bedroom than married people do?

Chapter VI   In This Corner We Have . . .

1. From the Bible, read Mark 14:43-72. How did Jesus handle conflict? How did Judas and Peter cope with it?
2. Have you had both "good" fights and "bad" fights? What seems to be the difference?

Chapter VII   The Bible and Woman's Lib

1. From the Bible, read Ephesians 5:21-33. Compare with I Peter 3:1-7 in the book. Do you agree with this interpretation of marriage?
2. The author and his wife believe that a woman secretly wants the man to exercise leadership, even though she often resists it. Do you think this argument is true?

Chapter VIII   For Everything There Is a Season

1. Do you have periodic times to be together -alone?
2. Do you have periodic times when you need total "aloneness"?
3. Can love and joy spring up out of suffering? Have they ever in your marriage experience?

Chapter IX   Love Story Reborn

1. What marriage therapy work is going on in your community? Is it adequate?
2. What preventive medicine is taking place to enrich marriages and help them grow?
3. What part does the Christian faith and the church play in strengthening (or weakening) your marriage?

Notes

Chapter I

1 Julian Huxley, *Look* (July 12, 1955), 21-29.
2 Erik H. Erikson, *Childhood and Society*, 2nd ed. rev. (New York: W. W. Norton & Co., 1963), p. 263.
3 Ernest Hemingway, *For Whom the Bell Tolls* (New York: Charles Scribner's Sons, 1940), p. 169.

Chapter II

1 Reuel Howe, *The Miracle of Dialogue* (New York: The Seabury Press, 1963), p. 3.
2 Ralph Waldo Emerson, *Friendship* (Westwood, N.J.. Fleming H. Revell, n.d.), pp. 30-32.
3 Howard J. Clinebell and Charlotte H. Clinebell, *The Intimate Marriage* (New York: Harper & Row, 1970), p. 81.
4 Carl Sandburg, *Honey and Salt* (New York: Harcourt, Brace, & World, 1963), p. 36. Used by permission.

Chapter III

1 Theodore Reik, *Listening with the Third Ear* (New York: Farrar, Straus, and Co., 1949).
2 Douglas Steere, *On Listening to Another* (New York: Harper & Row, 1955), p. 6.
3 Robert Raines, *Creative Brooding* (New York: The Macmillan Co., 1966), pp. 23-24 [emphasis mine].
4 Beatles, "Eleanor Rigby."

Chapter IV

1 James Kavanaugh, *There Are Men Too Gentle to Live Among Wolves*. (Los Angeles: Nash Publishing Corporation, 1970), n. p.
2 Paul Tournier, *The Meaning of Gifts* (Richmond: John Knox Press, 1961).
3 Reuel Howe, *Man's Need and God's Action* (Greenwich, Conn.: The Seabury Press, 1953), p. 85.

Chapter V

1 John Charles Wynn, *Sermons on Marriage and Family Life* (Nashville: Abingdon Press, 1956), p. 129.
2 Karl Menninger, *Love Against Hate* (New York: Harcourt, Brace, and Company, 1942), p. 48.
3 *Ibid.*, p. 49.
4 Vernard Eller, *Sex Manual for Puritans* (Nashville: Abingdon Press, 1971), pp. 53-54.
5 Max Levin, from a speech given to family doctors (*Kansas City Star*, fall, 1967).

Chapter VI

1 George Bach and Peter Wyden, *The Intimate Enemy* (New York: Avon Books, 1968).
2 *Ibid.*, p. 18.
3 Judith Viorst, *It's Hard to Be Hip over Thirty* (New York: New American Library [1968]), pp. 39-41.
4 Eric Berne, *Games People Play* (New York: Grove Press, 1964).

Chapter VII

1 Robert F. Capon, *Bed & Board: Plain Talk About Marriage* (New York: Simon & Schuster, 1970).

Chapter VIII

1 Charlie W. Shedd, *Letters to Karen* (New York: Avon Books, 1965), p. 53.
2 Kahlil Gibran, *The Prophet* (New York: Alfred A. Knopf, 1961), p. 15. Used by permission.
3 Ann Morrow Lindbergh, *Gift from the Sea* (New York: Pantheon Books, 1955), pp. 23, 30, 44.
4 Betty Jarmusch, "Down with Dialog," *Marriage Magazine*, December, 1971, p. 18.
5 Howard Whitman, *Philadelphia Sunday Bulletin*, January 15, 1967.
6 Kahlil Gibran, *The Prophet*, p. 29.

Chapter IX

1 *The Book of Worship* (Nashville: The United Methodist Publishing House, 1968).
2 Reuel Howe, *The Miracle of Dialogue*, p. 3.
3 Urban Steinmetz, *Marriage Enrichment Program* (Escanaba, Michigan, Family Life Bureau, 1965).
4 Quoted in Eleanor B. Luckey and George W. Wise, *Human Growth and the Family* (Nashville: Graded Press, 1970), p. 41.
5 Judith Viorst, *It's Hard to Be Hip over Thirty*, p. 25.